Nashville Baseball History:
From Sulphur Dell to the Sounds

Nashville Baseball History: From Sulphur Dell to the Sounds

By Bill Traughber

SUMMER
GAME
BOOKS

Portions of this book were published previously with local Nashville media
outlets.

ISBN: 978-1-938545-83-2 (print)
ISBN: 978-1-938545-84-9 (ebook)

For information about permissions, bulk purchases,
or additional distribution, write to
Summer Game Books
P. O. Box 818
South Orange, NJ 07079

or contact the publisher at
www.summergamebooks.com

Front cover images, left to right, top: Buck Showalter, Bob Lennon, and John
Wasdin. Below: Sulphur Dell, 1908.

To my grandsons Trip and Rhett,
whom I'm very proud of and love very much.

Acknowledgments

This project could not be as successful without the help of many people. My first gratitude goes to Charlie Miller the former managing editor of *Athlon Sports*. When I worked for *Athlon*, I took a trip to Cooperstown, N.Y., to research for a feature story on the National Baseball Hall of Fame and Museum that I would eventually write.

That was my first story ever published. I never had any formal training as a writer and always considered myself a researcher than a writer, but with Charlie's aid and support I became both.

The late Tom Squires, editor of *Nashville Sports Weekly* and *Titans Exclusive*, allowed me to submit Nashville sports history stories that in the beginning were rough and needed work. With his suggestions and patience my writing attempts improved to where I was a regular contributor to his publications. I don't believe I would have had success as a Nashville sports history writer without Tom's encouragement.

I would like to thank Nashville Sounds Vice-President, Operations Doug Scopel who allowed me to research and write a weekly Nashville baseball history story for the Sounds website and programs since 2004. I am in my 14th year as a freelance writer for the Sounds. Doug was honored by *Minor League News* as the 2006 P.R. Director of the Year, receiving the Ralphie Award that is presented to the top professional media relations' director.

More thanks to Ken Fieth and his staff at the Metro Archives; the staff at the Nashville Public Library (the Nashville Room); Philip Nagy and Henry Shipman of the Vanderbilt Archives; the National Baseball Hall of Fame and Library in Cooperstown, N.Y.; Allen Forkum editor of *Nashville Retrospect*, Larry Schmittou, Kyle Parkinson, Linda Center, Alex Wassell, Michael

Whitty, Eric Jones, Lulu Clark, Leanne Garland, Mike Strasinger, Paul Clements, Patty Sue Whitson and Skip Nipper.

Special thanks goes to Jeremy Jones for sharing part of his impressive Nashville baseball memorabilia collection that is the source of several illustrations for this project. And to Farrell Owens who wrote the heartfelt foreword to this book. I have always referred to Farrell as Nashville's "Mr. Baseball" due to his passion and devotion to the game. I believe if Farrell had the power he would replace the National Anthem with "Take Me Out to the Ballgame." Farrell contributed to the efforts to bring professional baseball and the Sounds to Nashville.

Congratulations to those lovable Chicago Cubs for winning the 2016 World Series, their first since 1908. Baseball's long national pastime nightmare is finally over. And congratulations to Vanderbilt baseball Coach Tim Corbin for being named the 2014 National Coach of the Year and his Commodores team for winning the College World Series that season. Corbin and his "Vandy Boys" also made it to the CWS finals the next season.

Contents

Part II: Great Players, Great Teams, Great Events

Part III. Nashville Sounds: The Tradition Grows

Contents

Foreword

It is an honor to write this foreword for my friend Bill Traughber, whose new book and well-researched feature stories from the past have re-introduced the wonderful history of Nashville baseball to many people. For me, the game of baseball has been at the core of my life since I was a young boy. Still today the passion and love I have for the game burns within me. It seems like yesterday when I was walking up 5th Avenue with my dad to enter the big rolled-back fences of Sulphur Dell.

One of my earliest memories that cemented my love for baseball was on May 8, 1959. My dad, who taught me about baseball, had taken me to Sulphur Dell, a Nashville Baseball Shrine, to watch the beloved Nashville Vols play. On this pleasant Friday night the most exciting thing that was happening at the ballpark for me was listening to the screeching wheels of the trains rolling by outside the ballpark as they made their way through Nashville.

After falling behind early, the Vols found themselves trailing the Memphis Chicks, 7-0 going into the bottom of the ninth. While many fans had left or were leaving, my dad encouraged my uncle and me to stay since Memphis was the class of the league. As the bottom of the Nashville line-up led off the final inning, little did I know I was going to witness history! Buddy Gilbert's leadoff single was followed by Phil Shartzer's double. Then Haven Schmidt excited the crowd with a pinch-hit, three-run, opposite field home run that hit the top of the leftfield fence and bounced over. At that point we were happy we wouldn't be shut out as then Carlos Castillo, Tommy Dotterer and Marv Blalock all singled, making the score 7-4.

After Crawford Davidson singled to load the bases, Chico Alvarez singled making it a two-run game. At that point you could feel something magical was going to happen in Nashville on this night. In ironic fashion, Nashville Vols catcher, Eddie Irons, strolled to the plate with the bases loaded and hit a hard line shot at the centerfielder. As the centerfielder took a half step in, the ball sailed over his head allowing three runs to score on Iron's triple, giving Nashville an unbelievable 8-7 win.

My love for baseball was heightened on this night because of the improbable rally that saw all eight runs scored with no outs, on nine straight hits. There were no walks, no errors and no hit batters during Nashville's miraculous inning. I couldn't imagine a more magical night at Sulphur Dell.

Growing up and playing in Nashville's summer baseball program that had such a rich history will always be a great memory. Summer baseball was at an all-time high in both number and competition as the game was in full force in Nashville. Playing for Coursey's BBQ and coaching the Haury and Smith team in the City and Tri-State Leagues are cherished times, along with playing baseball with some of my lifelong friends at Cohn High School and later David Lipscomb College.

It was my honor to play for the legendary Ken Dugan at Lipscomb, where he built the Bisons into one of the finest programs in the country. I had a front row seats to watch the great Lipscomb and Vanderbilt games in the 1970s where over 5,000 fans would circle Lipscomb's Onion Dell to watch these historical battles.

After the Nashville Vols organization came to a close in 1963 and Sulphur Dell was demolished in 1969, professional baseball went silent for fifteen years. It was October, 1976 when the telephone rang, and on the other end of the line was my friend and Vanderbilt head baseball coach Larry Schmittou. He wanted to meet me in the press box at the Babe Ruth Baseball Field in Bellevue.

This meeting was the beginning of a new professional baseball team coming to Nashville. In December 1976 Larry and I found ourselves at the Winter Baseball meetings at the Hilton Hotel in Los Angeles soliciting every professional baseball team to meet with us in our hotel room to discuss professional baseball returning to Nashville.

To say we were anxious was a major understatement, and finally we had one, and only one, knock at the door. When we opened the door, in walked Sheldon "Chief" Bender, Farm Director of the Cincinnati Reds who was interested in coming to Nashville. With the financial backing of the Hershel Greer estate and Mr. Greer's son, Lynn, and the support of Metro Parks Director's Charlie Spears and Jim Fyke, we secured the old Ft. Negley Baseball Field to establish what would become Herschel Greer Stadium.

The Kats, Pickers, Stars, Vols and Sounds were all on the voting list as potential names. When the votes were tallied from select sports writers, country music entertainers and others the new ball club would be the Nashville Sounds. A big blessing on the opening night was a rainout that allowed us to secure the backstop netting to resurrect professional baseball in Nashville.

The early years at Greer were absolutely crazy, with record crowds, wacky promotions, and country music entertainers performing. Greer Stadium had become the place to be seen if you were a star in Nashville. Some of the most cherished memories were meeting George Steinbrenner, Mickey Mantle, Whitey Ford, Sparky Anderson, Yogi Berra, Johnny Bench and countless other baseball icons and Nashville's top brass. Then, in 1979 when the team captured the Southern League Championship, we knew baseball was here to stay.

For me personally, I am rounding third base and heading home, and I cherish each baseball game I attend. The game might be at Seven Oaks, Shelby Park, or an unnamed Little League Field, but it is enjoyable to watch this game we once played and now love to watch. The greatest memory baseball in Nashville has given me is the countless friendships that I have had over the years and will continue to have hopefully many more years.

I couldn't wait to be in the stands on opening night at Nashville's new Baseball Shrine (First Tennessee Park) and hear the crack of the bat and see little kids carrying their gloves in anticipation for that foul ball that they know will come their way. I looked forward to that moment when the Nashville Sounds make a big comeback and I think back on that special night with my dad in 1959 at Sulphur Dell. But the real icing on the cake will be late in the game when I hear that same sound of that train rolling across the tracks outside the ballpark. At that moment I will know I am only a Texas Leaguer away from where I was sitting years ago, and know while time marches on, some things have remained the same.

Put me in Coach, I'm ready to play!

Farrell Owens

Nashville Sounds General Manager (1978-82)

David Lipscomb University Athletics Hall of Fame (Class of 1992)

39-year Board Member of the Nashville Baseball Old Timers Association

Preface

As a child, I grew up with the desire to be a major league baseball player for my team the Baltimore Orioles. I do not recall how I became an Orioles' fan. I was a fan before the Orioles' stunning World Series victory over the Dodgers in 1966—a four-game sweep. My mother told me when I was little I would sing, and that she called me her "Oriole." I do not know if that stuck in my toddler brain, but I have been a devoted Orioles fan since that time.

I did play Little League Baseball for our team sponsor "Associates Finance." We played our games in Madison, where I learned about "warming the bench." The next year I played for McKinnon Bridge Co., in my grammar school. I started, but my only highlight was hitting a home run on the fenced field that was located in what is now the parking lot behind Greer Stadium. It was the only home run that year for the team, so I can honestly say I led McKinnon Bridge Co. in dingers. My twin brother, Gill, was the pitcher and I was the catcher.

That was it for me as a baseball player, but I continued to follow the Orioles and the great game of baseball, as I do to this day. Later in my life I became a freelance writer of Nashville sports history. My first introduction to the Nashville Vols baseball team (1901-1962, 1963) came from George Leonard, the senior editor at *Athlon Sports* where I once worked. George had been an editor for the *Nashville Banner* and after retiring there he finished his career at *Athlon*.

For a long time, George was the Vols beat writer for the *Banner*. He gave me a booklet he co-wrote with legendary sports writer Fred Russell on the Vols' first fifty years. George would tell me stories of Sulphur Dell, the Vols' old home ballpark. He told me about the ballpark's strange dimensions and the embankment along the outfield fence.

My first interview with a former Nashville Vols' player was Bob Lennon, who told me about hitting 64 home runs for the Vols in 1954. Later I met with the popular Buster Boguskie at his home. The former Vols' second baseman tied a Southern Association record with six hits in a game, which he accomplished in the 1948 season-opener at Sulphur Dell. I was honored to receive a letter from former Vols and Yankees' pitcher Johnny Sain, letting me know how much he enjoyed speaking with me about playing in Nashville and for his manager Larry Gilbert. As a team historian, I have interviewed several other Nashville Vols, all of whom enjoyed playing baseball in the city.

Along the way I expanded my baseball research into the 19th century, and discovered that the professional game began in Nashville with the Americans (1885-86), followed by the Blues (1887), Tigers (1893-94), Seraphs (1895) and Centennials (1897). Baseball was played on the Sulphur Dell site as early as 1866. Though the origin of Nashville baseball is not known, I did learn that the earliest known documentations of baseball in the city can be found in newspaper articles in 1857 and 1860, debunking the belief that the citizens of Nashville were taught the game by the occupying Union Army during the Civil War.

Much of my research is done through the old city newspapers on microfiche in the Nashville Public Library. It is greatly satisfying to discover and retell stories about players and games that stretch as far back as 150 years ago. Sports writers in those early years had an interesting and unique writing style. I like to use their descriptive words in my stories, since they were there and can tell it the best.

It can be time-consuming searching through microfiche rolls, but it is time well spent when you make a discovery like a night baseball game played in Nashville in 1894. What a thrill it was to be the first person to tell that story in more than 100 years! The early days of Nashville baseball were filled with arguments with umpires, brawls, and other adventures that typified the early days of baseball. Championships hung in the balance when some of these late-season battles occurred.

Numerous all-time baseball greats have played in Nashville, ever since Hall of Famer Cap Anson brought his Chicago White Stockings to Nashville for a three-week spring training period in 1885. A young Cy Young pitched a game in Sulphur Dell in 1895 when he was playing with the Cleveland Spiders. Other baseball greats to play in Nashville include Christy Mathewson, Honus Wagner, manager Connie Mack and his Athletics, Tris Speaker, Babe Ruth, Lou Gehrig, Joe DiMaggio, Ted Williams, Mickey Mantle, Jackie Robinson, Hank Aaron, Reggie Jackson, and Eddie Murray, along with many others.

Nashville baseball history includes told stories about the Southern Association Vols, a lawsuit to prevent Sunday baseball (1911), a perfect game (1916), the heritage of black ballplayers, the city hosting All-Star games, championship teams, and a vice-president tossing the ceremonial first pitch.

Baseball in Nashville did not stop with the demolition of Sulphur Dell in 1969. The Nashville Sounds continued the city's baseball legacy joining the Southern League in 1978 and they remain one of the top minor league franchises today. Owner Larry Schmittou built Herschel Greer Stadium that has hosted three championship teams in Double-A and Triple-A. Bringing fans to the ballpark were players like Steve Balboni, Don Mattingly, Willie McGee, Buck Showalter, Skeeter Barnes, Tike Redman, Aramis Ramirez, Corey Hart, Prince Fielder and R.A. Dickey.

A new era of Sounds baseball began in 2015 with the completion of a new downtown ballpark—First Tennessee Park.

Few cities that have not been home to a major league team can boast such a rich, diverse baseball history as Nashville, Tennessee!

PART I

The Early Years

The Origins of Nashville Baseball

The origin of Nashville baseball is not documented, but it is a myth that Union soldiers taught the citizens of the city to play the game during the Civil War with their occupation in early 1862. It was unlikely that spirited Confederates would be playing games with the the their northern enemy. A newspaper article in the July 1860 issue of the *Republican Banner* describes a game of baseball being observed from downtown Nashville. It read:

Base Ball. —This healthful and exciting exercise was generally popular last fall, especially in the Northern States, and we hope it will be introduced here as soon as the heated term passes off. We noticed the other evening a party engaged in Base Ball on the Edgefield side of the river, all apparently enjoying themselves. The early closing of the stores gives a fine opportunity to the young men engaged in mercantile pursuits.

No better exercise can be indulged in. The difference between Base Ball and the exercises of the gymnasium is so obvious that we need scarcely mention it. In the former, not only every muscle of the body is brought into active play, but the desire to win produces a healthy excitement of the mental faculties, without which any sort of physical exercise is not only useless but positively injurious. On the other hand, in ordinary gymnastic exercises, the mental incentive is entirely wanting, and the so-called gymnastic exercise is simply reduced to ex-labor.

Let us have Base Ball Clubs organized, then and the fun commenced.

That game was played on the eastern side of the Cumberland River in the Edgefield community. This was before the Civil War and the election of Abraham Lincoln.

The first known mention of baseball in the city is documented in a November 1857 article in the *Nashville Daily News* with the heading "The Hickory Club:"

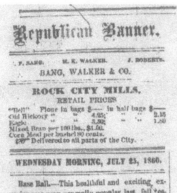

This article in the July 25, 1860 *Republican Banner*, is one the earliest known documentations of Nashville baseball. *Courtesy of the author.*

This is the name of an association recently organized in this city, having for its object the physical and mental improvement of its members. The club is composed principally of young men, though there are also a considerable number of those of riper years attached to it. It is proposed to adapt the practice of mainly athletics, out door games such as Cricket, Baseball, etc., and to have...a debating Society, Reading Room and Library.

There is no record that any baseball games were played by this association.

An area of downtown in North Nashville (Sulphur Bottom) near Fourth and Fifth Avenues was a gathering spot for the early pioneers to trade, gather water and picnicking. The area also contained a sulphur spring that was used for medicinal purposes. It was not uncommon to see deer and buffalo roaming the area. This was a natural place to build a ballpark, which was known as Sulphur Springs Bottom (later Athletic Park and Sulphur Dell).

After the Civil War baseball gained popularity in Nashville and the South. The *Nashville Gazette* reported in its August 1, 1866 edition:

A match game of base ball for the championship of the South between the Louisville Club, of Louisville Ky., and the Cumberland, of this city, took place yesterday afternoon, resulting in the triumph of the former. Both sides showed great skill in the game and the visitors were generous enough in awarding a great degree of proficiency to their unfortunate competitors. The uniform of the Cumberland was white shirts with broad lapels, blue pantaloons and white and blue caps.

Louisville won 39 to 23 at Fort Gillem (Fisk University site). Fort Gillem was one of the Union Army's forts that were scattered around Nashville. More of the early games documented in Nashville are traced to September 1867. The Nashville Club played the Phoenix Club in a two-of-three series for the championship of Davidson County.

The Phoenix team won the series in three games. A box score of the second game revealed a Nashville victory, 58-29. The series did not end without controversy. Baseball fans from that era revealed their team loyalty and emotions in the same manner as modern fans.

One part of baseball exhibited by a Nashvillian reveals the fan's passion for his team. A few days after the Phoenix team's victory, a fan, using the name "A. Ball," sent a letter to the editor, which was printed in the Sept. 27, 1867 edition of the *Republican Banner* and it read in part:

A match game was played Tuesday between the Nashville and Phoenix Baseball Clubs, which was witnessed by a large number of spectators, with but little satisfaction however.

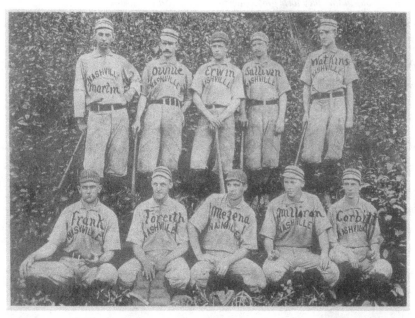

The 1887 Nashville Maroons were organized in 1868 and became one of the top amateur clubs in the city. *Robert S. Corbitt photograph.*

Quite a discussion was held between the friends of both clubs. It was generally agreed that there was unfairness exhibited on the part of the Umpire, Mr. Wm. Buck.

The following items by a "spectator" will prove the above. Mr. F. Gault of the Phoenix was on the first base and endeavored to make the second---he passed the second, during which a foul was called. Instead of returning to the second base, and touching it, he crossed the diamond and reached the first base thus violating the 23rd section of the rules and regulations of National Association of Base Ball Clubs.

And into the 21st century umpires still can't get a break. "Mr. Ball" wrote word for word from the rule book stating in detail the runner has to touch second base on his way back to first. He can't take a shortcut. The runner should have been called out, but wasn't. This was the cause for "Mr. Ball's." disdain. He gave other violations of the rulebook against the Nashville Club.

The dissatisfied Nashville fan continued:

Partiality was exhibited throughout the entire game, and everything went in favor of the Phoenix. It was not thought by the spectators that the game would be claimed by Capt. Sullivan: but in this they were grossly deceived. Capt. Sullivan, himself admitted that they was marked unfairness and partiality on the part of the Umpire.

Capt. Sullivan was, J. W. Sullivan, the Vice-President of the Phoenix Club. Apparently, Mr. Sullivan was a *Republican Banner* subscriber as the next day's edition printed his rebuttal in a letter to the editor:

The communication published in your paper yesterday over the signature of "A. Ball," was manifestly partial. Although claimed to have been written by a spectator, I think it owes it paternity to some member of the Nashville Club, or to a zealous partisan.

The first statement that "It was generally agreed that it was unfairness exhibited on the part of the Umpire," will no doubt, astonish a large majority of the spectators as it does me. The idea must have originated in the fertile imagination of "A. Ball," as I have never heard it mentioned except by some member of the club in whose interests he writes.

In justice to Mr. Buck I would state, that no Umpire had been selected previous to the hour for playing, and in the name of all that is reasonable, why did not the Nashville Club object to that gentleman before the game began, instead of accusing him of partiality at it's close?

Mr. Sullivan continued his letter disputing some of "Mr. Ball's," facts while admitting the umpire missed some calls. However, he steadfastly stood by his team by continuing:

In conclusion, permit me to say in behalf of the Phoenix, that it is our aim to promote the cultivation of kindly feelings among the different Base-Ball Clubs.

"That we think we fairly won the championship of Davidson County, and have the champion-bat in our possession and intend to retain it until vanquished in a square, stand-up fight in an open field when we will yield it cheerfully and gracefully, but never through a newspaper controversy.

Perhaps Mr. A. Ball's opinion inspired some passions for the organized game of baseball in Nashville, as expressed by an editorial in the October 22, 1867 edition of the *Nashville Daily Press & Times*.

There is something a little wonderful in the enthusiasm which our "national game" has excited among all classes of people, in all parts of our country. Beginning in our eastern cities, it rapidly became popular, and organizations sprang up with the facility of mushrooms, until no village or hamlet in the country, east or west [or south-Author], was without its base ball club.

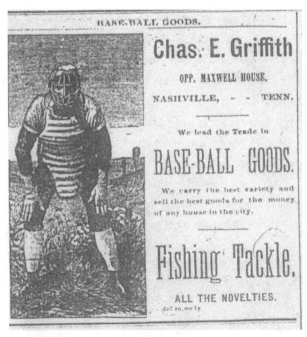

This newspaper ad for a sporting goods company appeared in the May 3, 1885 edition of the *Daily American. Courtesy of the author.*

Young men were fascinated with the sport; older men encouraged it as promotion of hard muscles and a good digestion. Teachers of morals rejoiced that an amusement had been found which broke none of the commandments and permitted the spiritual sapling to pursue a perpendicular growth.

Merchants, bankers, and shopkeepers closed their establishments, and gave their clerks a holiday on a Saturday afternoon, that they might drive dyspepsia from their cadaverous eyes. The ladies lent the magnetism of their presence to the game, and through blistering hours exposed their carefully nursed complexions to the bronzing sun in their eagerness to witness the skill and prowess of their brothers and lovers.

One powerful amateur baseball club were the Nashville Maroons organized in 1868. Other amateur teams included Arlington, Pioneer, Montgomery Bell, Old Zeke, the Phoenix Club, Nashville Athletic Club, Cumberland, the East Nashville Deppins, Stonewall, Lone Star, Crockett, Burns, Flynn, Pontiac, Rock City, the North Nashville Juniors and Linck's Hotel.

The year 1885 was the beginning of professional baseball in Nashville. The original Southern League (1885-89, 1892-96, 1898-99) was formed with the Nashville Americans as a charter member. The Nashville newspapers covered the team and league with detailed scores and reports. The Americans played for only two seasons (1985-86), while the city was later represented in the league by the Nashville Blues (1887), Nashville Tigers (1893-94), and the Nashville Seraphs (1895).

The Southern League folded after the 1899 season. The league would rebound in 1901 as the Southern Association, fielding a Nashville club as a charter member. Eventually named the Vols (short for Volunteers), Nashville would field a team from 1901-61 and 1963. The South Atlantic League (known as the Sally League) changed its name to the Southern League in 1964 and added the Nashville Sounds to its membership in 1978.

Sulphur Springs Bottom

With professional baseball arriving in Nashville in 1885, more amateur teams and leagues were being formed so the city needed to improve and make additions to the Sulphur Springs Bottom ballpark. The March 21, 1885 issue of the *Daily Union* reports on the ambitious project of the renovation. You will notice that the ballpark is referred to as an amphitheatre:

The descriptions hitherto published have done meager justice to the improvements now in progress in the Sulphur Springs bottom. Visitors are surprised at the wonderful changes that have been made in this hitherto neglected portion of the city. The three sections of the amphitheatre are now nearing completion. Yesterday the seats were being laid and in four or five days this work will be finished. The erection of the great fence has begun, and Monday the force will be put to work grading the grounds.

The Cherry St. amphitheatre is 150 feet long. The middle section 74 feet. The main entrance is directly off Jackson St. into the main section of the amphitheatre. To the right of this large door is the ticket seller's office formed by a small projection of the Cherry St. side. The passageway from the entrance opens into the amphitheatre at the middle row of the seats. This section will be reserved for ladies and their escorts. The chairs will be backed, armed and nicely cushioned. The diamond will be directly in front of the reserve seats, which will be protected from wild balls by a high screen, with meshes two and one half inches square. Polite ushers will be in attendance on the ladies.

In the late 1800's, Fourth Ave. N. was Cherry St., while Fifth Ave. was Summer St. The "ballpark" was being built in consideration of utilizing other sporting events. A track was constructed 150 yards in circumference around the outfield for bicycling and a running. It was reported that one outfield fence was 362 feet and another 485 feet. Also noted was the fact that the

This sketch of the Sulphur Springs Bottom baseball park appeared in the Union newspaper on March 18, 1886. *Courtesy of the author.*

long distances would, "be almost impossible to knock the ball over the fence anywhere even if it weren't so high."

Since the ballpark would attract a large number of people parking was taken into consideration. An enclosure was built along the Summer St. side for fans to park their "horses and carriages."

Other accommodations were also taken care of as, "this house will contain a circular counter with four fountains to which by hydraulic pressure, the sulphur water will be pumped from the spring below. It is a large roomy building and will be a delightful resort. It will also contain bath-rooms, the water possessing excellent quantities for this purpose."

More additions were reported:

Underneath the main amphitheatre will be rooms for the players, directors, scorers and reporters. Two rooms will face the diamond, the large opening partitioned by a wire screen. In one the reporters and scorers will sit, and all the others will be reserved for the directors.

Taking it all in all, the grounds for extent and conveniences will not be surpassed by any in the country. Already Manager Bryan is receiving such offers from such shows as the "Wild West" to rent to grounds for their exhibitions.

On Thanksgiving Day in 1885, the ballpark hosted Nashville's first organized football game with the Nashville Football Club defeating the Nashville Athletic Club, 6-4.

Legendary sportswriter Grantland Rice is responsible for the ballpark name change from Sulphur Springs Bottom to Sulphur Dell. In the mid-1880's the ballpark was mostly referred to as Athletic Park. Rice in his *Tennessean* column from January 14, 1908 wrote in part:

"With his arrival, too, the saw and the hammer get busy reclaiming the arid waste Sulphur Spring, which classic spot, with a new set of stands, will be known as Sulphur Spring Dell, and not Sulphur Spring Bottom, as of yore."

In his columns, Rice eventually began shortening the name to Sulphur Dell. *Nashville Banner* sports writer Fred Russell once wrote that Rice changed the name to accommodate his poetic style of sports writing as he found more words to rhyme with "Dell" than "Bottom."

The 1885 Nashville Americans

As a charter member of the Southern League, Atlanta, Augusta, Macon, Columbus, Memphis, Chattanooga and Birmingham joined the Nashville Americans.

Nashville was also the 1885 spring training camp for the Chicago White Stockings. Hall of Famer Cap Anson led his club to Nashville for a three-week period at Sulphur Springs Bottom (also Athletic Park). The ballpark was located near a sulphur spring.

Anson, a pioneer in baseball and 1939 Hall of Fame inductee, was the White Stockings player/manager. The White Stockings would win the National League pennant with an 87-25 record later that fall. It was suggested that the waters of Sulphur Bottom "energized" the Chicagoans to victory.

Americans' exhibition games were played with Chicago, local amateur clubs and Vanderbilt University. Sulphur Springs Park was the Americans home field. The players of this era generally received $50 to $60 a month while the pitchers and catchers might earn a little more. The distance from the pitcher to the catcher was 50 feet. The bases were 90 feet apart, but the bases on first and third were positioned outside the lines. The next year, the bases were moved inside the lines.

The catchers did have protection, but nothing close to what you see in modern baseball. They stood several feet behind the batter. The single umpire would position himself several feet behind the catcher. His accuracy in calling balls and strikes was a point of frustration for players and fans. The umpire would move himself behind the pitcher when there was a base runner. Umpires were also given the power to dish out fines on the spot, as the Nashville Americans would experience.

The 1885 Nashville Americans were charter members of the newly formed Southern League. *Courtesy of Skip Nipper.*

Seven balls had to be taken before a batter would be given a free trip to first base. However, in 1885, the batters could tell the pitcher to throw strikes high or low. Another rule that lasted only a year enabled the batter to use a bat that was flat on one side.

Accurate statistics and records from that era are unavailable and incomplete. The newspapers of that day would refer to a player with his last name. Occasionally, in a feature story the players' and umpire's full names were given. For this story, some first names will be omitted.

Nashville's opening-day lineup for 1885 included: Leonard Sowders, first base; James Hillery, third base; John Cullen, second base; Joe Werrick, shortstop; Alexander Voss, pitcher; George Rhue, left field; Joe Diestel, center field; Tony Hellman, catcher and William Bryan, right field. Bryan was also Nashville's manager. Player/managers were common during this era.

Prior to opening day, exhibition games were played with various ball teams throughout the South. Nashville's morning newspaper, *The Daily American,* gave this report on the city's anticipated first organized professional baseball

Baseball pioneer Cap Anson brought his Chicago White Stockings to Nashville in 1885 for spring training. *Courtesy of the National Baseball Hall of Fame and Library, Cooperstown, New York.*

game played in Nashville on May 4, 1885.

This afternoon at 3:30 o'clock the first Nashville game in the Southern League championship season will be played at the new base ball park between the Americans and the Columbus Club.

The locals have for several weeks past been on their first Southern trip of the season, and in the face o' bad luck with some of their own players and the horrible umpiring system, have in most instances made highly credible records. They deserve a large attendance and a perfect ovation at the hands of Nashville people.

They have made friends wherever they have visited and return a close second to the highest yet made by a club that has been playing off its own grounds. The Columbus club is considered by Manager Schmelz of the Atlantas, and also Manager Bryan, of the Americans, to be one of the strongest in the league, and the game this afternoon will undoubtedly be full of interest.

Nashville lost that first game to Columbus 3-2. During this period the home team had the option of batting first or last in an inning. The home team generally batted first. Hillery, batting second, got Nashville's first hit in the first inning. Sowders led off the inning reaching first base on an error. Cullen also reached base in the first inning on an error. Werrick followed with a triple, scoring Hillery and Cullen for the Americans' only runs of the game.

Scanning the newspapers from throughout the season, a July incident in Nashville involved an umpire and a questionable call. The game with Columbus was tied 4-4 when Nashville came to bat in the ninth. With two out, Diestel and W. T. Crowell were on first and second base. Charles Marr followed with a hit between left and centerfielder.

Crowell scored and Diestel slid into home plate obviously ahead of the throw from the outfield. However, the umpire called a "slide out." The umpire claimed that Diestel had run out of the "three-foot line" and was therefore out. Nat Kellogg, who was catching for Nashville, protested the call and Umpire McCue fined him $10 on the spot. Diestel and Sneed of Nashville also complained, and they were instantly fined $5 each. Columbus scored in their half of the ninth to win, 5-4.

The Daily American gave this report of the incident:

The spectators had seen, in the previous game, exhibitions of McCue's puffiness and were thoroughly indignant at him for robbing them of their game. When the players came in Diestel walked up to McCue in a threatening manner and denounced him for calling him out when he was perfectly safe. If it had not been for the ladies in the grand stand Diestel would have hit him. By this time an angry-looking mob came pilling down from the amphitheater, and it looked very much like black eyes, tar and feathers, or something worst for McCue.

Manager Mayberry, in the meanwhile, seemed to have anticipated something of the kind, and hurried a number of police down into the diamond to protect the poor unfortunate McCue. They arrived on the spot in good time. The gang of spectators were about to administer to him what they evidently believed deserved, when he met with his timely rescue. After going to his room to get his coat he was escorted by a body guard of police out of the grounds up Cherry Street to Gaffney's saloon on Church Street. Several hundred people, many of whom were negroes and small boys followed him the entire distance. Upon the streets the umpire, his foul decisions and general incompetency were the talk of everybody.

McCue went to his room at Linck's Hotel and said he intended to umpire the next day's game. He also said that if there were any "guying or hooting in the audience or by players, he would fire the whole crowd from the park." Diestel and Sneed confronted McCue at the hotel where McCue informed the ball players that their fine was now $10 and not the original $5.

Mayberry was reportedly the Nashville manager at this time. That night Mayberry, along with the Columbus manager, telegraphed the league office to request McCue's dismissal as an umpire. Other complaints appeared such as "he is the only umpire in the South who has sent batters to base because the pitcher 'unnecessarily delayed' the game." It was also reported that of

Outfielder Charles Marr played for the Nashville Americans for two seasons and earned the 1886 Southern League batting title (.327). *Courtesy of the National Baseball Hall of Fame and Library, Cooperstown, New York.*

the 16 fines imposed by the umpires that season in the Southern League, 12 were by McCue.

The next day McCue was sent a telegraph from the league office informing him that he was fired due to incompetence.

Another incident that summer involved a rumor in Nashville that a special new player would be added to the roster. The game was in Nashville against Birmingham.

The newspaper gave the report:

The mysterious man who had been signed by the locals, it transpired was a huge joke. He was none other than the negro Mascot, who was gaudily attired for the occasion in a suit of red with the word "Mascot" on the back of his shirt and "Nashvilles" on the front, while a large sunflower glowed on his breasts. He was put up to bat to the applause of the grandstand, and after two strikes had been called hit to second base. The visitors were in on the joke, and by laughable errors allowed him to score.

The Civil War had ended just 20 years earlier and the prejudices against other races were strong. Blacks were allowed to attend the games, but were always seated in the "Negro bleachers." Newspapers' language was insensitive and insulting by today's standards. This reporting practice would continue well into the 20th century.

The largest crowd of that season in Nashville occurred Aug 29. Over 1,200 fans attended a special "Ladies Day." The Americans beat Augusta, 6-5. Another newspaper story revealed that in one game the Nashville club wore their "old gold uniforms, which have been fixed up, so that they are undoubtedly the most striking suits in the league."

The Americans placed third in the final standings of that inaugural 1885 season with a record of 62-39. Atlanta won the pennant with a 66-32 record. Sowders was the league's first batting champion (.309). The following season Sowders played in the American Association (new major league rival of the National League) for Baltimore.

The Americans also fielded a team in 1886, finishing in third place with a 46-43 record, but folded after the season due to a poor financial situation. Charles Marr led Nashville and the Southern League in batting (.327) that season.

The 1887 Nashville Blues

In 1887, financial problems forced two-time league champion Atlanta to drop out of the Southern League along with Augusta, Macon and Chattanooga. Nashville was able to put together another team that became the Blues.

New Orleans and Mobile became replacement teams, joining Charleston, Memphis, Savannah, and Nashville for a six-team league. The revamped league would experiment in 1887 with new rules. The number of strikes was raised to four and base on balls would credit the batter with a hit. This experiment was dropped the next year as batting averages soared.

The season began for the Blues with a March exhibition series with the Syracuse Shamrocks at Sulphur Springs Bottom. George Bradley was the Blues manager and also played third base. Bradley had a 10-year major league career with several teams beginning in 1876 with St. Louis of the National League.

The highlight of the exhibition season was the arrival of the major league Detroit Wolverines to Nashville. Detroit finished the previous season in second place of the National League. They came in just three games behind Cap Anson's potent Chicago White Stockings. The Wolverines were described as, "The most powerful and the highest priced aggregation of base ball players in the world."

The Nashville morning newspaper, *The Daily American*, was so impressed with the Wolverines arrival in the city that they printed nearly a full-page story on the team. Sketches and profiles were included on 14 players and their manager Bill Watkins. Detroit would sweep the Blues 14-4, 8-0 and 12-2. Approximately 1,200 fans including "several women" witnessed the final game. Detroit would continue with their dominant ways and win the 1887 National League championship.

Detroit was a member of the National League from 1881-88. They became charter members of the newly formed American League in 1901 where they became the Tigers.

There was a report that before the second game of the series, Southern League president John Morrow led a contingent to the Belle Meade horse farm. Accompanying him in "Open carriages drawn by some of Tennessee's fastest horses" were the Blues team and visiting press representatives. Gen. William Jackson, the farm owner, entertained the group with refreshments and special viewings of his top horses Iroquois, Enquirer and Great Tom.

The Blues uniforms were described as "light blue shirts and pants, white

This photo of former Nashville Blues player/manager George Washington Bradley was taken in 1925 when he was 73 years old. *Courtesy of the National Baseball Hall of Fame and Library, Cooperstown, New York*

belts, red stockings and red and white caps." It was reported that the uniforms were made by A. J. Reach & Co., and "Also sent to the club their compliments a box of handsome toilet articles for the club dressing rooms."

The 1887 season would bring to Nashville a heated rivalry with Memphis and financial problems. Only one umpire was assigned to each game. Game times at Sulphur Springs Park would be in the afternoon at 2:30, 3:30 or 4:00 while bleacher seats were a 25 and 50 cents. The individual series with each league team would be four games and travel was, of course, by train.

The state of Tennessee had a law that banned the playing of baseball on Sundays. The Blues were advised to play their first scheduled Sunday game believing the law was unconstitutional. Just prior to the initial Sunday game, a meeting was held at the Y.M.C.A and attended by several Nashville ministers. The group wanted the law to be enforced. Petitions were to be circulated around town condemning the violation of the law.

The Sunday game was played before a large crowd without incident. However, later that week the Davidson County grand jury sent indictments to all the Nashville and Savannah players involved in the game. Also indicted were the officials of the Nashville Base Ball Association.

The law offices of Vertrees & Vertrees, Demoss & Malone were the attorneys representing the Nashville club. The lawyers must have been one of Nashville's best as they were able to have the charges dropped. Sunday baseball continued in Nashville that year.

A newspaper article also reported that the Square Street and Market Street nine would play a series for the city's championship. Final results were not located.

The Nashville Blues exploded to a 16-3 record early in the season. Mobile folded as a team after a 5-21 start, and two weeks later Savannah joined them. Birmingham was persuaded to field a team and join the league. The schedule had to be revised for the remaining portion of the season.

When the Blues were out of town, Nashvillians could gather at the downtown Masonic Theatre to learn game updates by telegraph.

At one game in Nashville it was reported that a young lady in the grand stand suggested, "That the names of the players be chalked on their backs for the benefit of the spectators." The lady had foresight. It would be decades before names were affixed to baseball jerseys. Numbers would not be in use for identification purposes until the 1920s.

Nashville's top pitcher was Al Maul (9-3). While rumors began to circulate that Nashville was in financial difficulty (again), they were forced to sell Maul to Philadelphia of the National League where he went 4-2. Maul played 15 years with 10 different teams in professional baseball. The Blues top hitter was first baseman Michael Firle (.322).

A scandalous event was reported in *The Daily American* concerning a Blues player. Blues pitcher Larry Corcoran was scheduled to pitch a Saturday game in Nashville against Memphis. An investigation revealed that Corcoran was intoxicated before the game. A Memphis player, Bob Black, reportedly was the culprit to have gotten Corcoran intoxicated so Memphis would win.

It was revealed that certain parties from Memphis had bet large amounts of money against Nashville. When manager Bradley learned of the scheme, he promptly replaced Corcoran on the mound himself and got the victory. Corcoran was fined $50 and suspended indefinitely. Also under investigation was Memphis manager John Sneed for his complicity. Corcoran was eventually sold to Indianapolis for $500.

Black would also have to leave his team after a July series in Nashville to testify in a Memphis murder case.

Sneed was a controversial man himself. Often he was fined as much as $100 for his "abusive language." Sneed was also under investigation for trying to break up the league. The Memphis officials tried to suspend him due to his irrational behavior. But, Sneed retained an attorney to keep his contract enforced. Later in the season he was sold to Indianapolis.

Al Maul was the Blues top pitcher with a 9-3 record. *Courtesy of the National Baseball Hall of Fame and Library, Cooperstown, New York.*

The Blues were eventually forced to sell off players during the season in order to remain stable financially. The turnover in the roster affected the team's record. They were losing much more often.

Nashville (32-32) finally did fold as a team during the first week in August. In withdrawing their franchise from the league they forfeited their $1,000 guarantee to complete the season. It was estimated that the Blues lost $18,000.

New Orleans would win the Southern League pennant (74-40) followed by Charleston (66-41) and Memphis (65-46).

Nashville would not rejoin the Southern League until 1893-94 when they became the Tigers.

Night Baseball in 1894!

The Nashville Vols have been credited with playing the city's first night baseball game on May 18, 1931. That game was held at the Sulphur Dell ballpark against Southern Association foe Mobile. This is not actually correct.

George Stallings was a player/manager for the 1894 Nashville Tigers playing in the outfield and catching. *Courtesy of Jeremy Jones.*

The Nashville Tigers, of the Southern League, played the first game by artificial light in the city. The July 4, 1894 edition of Nashville's *The Daily American*, boldly proclaimed in headlines, "BASE BALL BY ELECTRIC LIGHT!" and, "Grand Pyrotechnic Display."

More headlines in bold letters stated, "MOST NOVEL EXHIBITION EVER SEEN IN THE SOUTH!" That scheduled game was rained out twice, but was finally played as an exhibition on July 6. The New Orleans Pelicans were the opponents. The two teams had played a doubleheader during the afternoon with each team winning once.

The third game (50 cents admission, children-25 cents) was scheduled for 8:30 p.m. with several pre-game activities. The Nashville club was experiencing financial difficulties and the exhibition was a means to raise money.

It was reported that 54 large electric lights were scattered around the Athletic Park and a ball covered with phosphorus was used. The pre-game festivities included a brass band and fireworks. A gentleman, Mr. Wiles, entertained the estimated 4,000 fans with "novelty" handstands and a high wire walk. A typical Tigers home game in 1894 usually drew several hundred people.

Exhibitions of "long distance" throwing and sliding were displayed by some of the Tigers players. One of the players was George Stallings, who was also Nashville's manager in 1894. Stallings also participated in a series of 100-yard races against the New Orleans club's players. The newspaper reported that Nashville had the sprinters and Stallings, "Proved himself an expert in the business."

Another report stated that when it was time for the baseball game, the "spectators looked for the appearance of the players with breathless expectation, which changed to a roar of laughter when the teams marched on the field."

The players came onto the field two abreast wearing, "Characteristic costumes on the ridiculous order." This is how *The Daily American* described the Tigers costumes:

There was Johnnie O'Brien, true to his nationality, and nobody wants to mistake him if he did sport side whiskers and a high hat with the orthodox Irish suit of blue cutaway with shining buttons. "Skirts" Harper was there, too, with the cutest of feminine costumes on and from the shades of a modest bonnet there appeared a face adorned with a fierce moustache, while down to his shoulders fell a most venerable suit of gray curls.

O'Brien was Nashville's second baseman while Harper was a pitcher. Stallings was reported to have worn a ballet costume with a grass skirt. One of the players climbed one of the light poles while running the bases. This was truly was an exhibition game of shenanigans for the fans as Nashville capped the tripleheader winning, 3-2.

Photographs were not used in newspapers in that era, but sketches were printed. Sketches showed Stallings wearing a grass skirt; Harper in a dress and O'Brien in his fancy suit and hat.

One anonymous reporter gave the opinion that, "Ball playing by electric light is a dismal failure." He failed to provide reasons.

Shortstop Pete Sweeney led the 1894 Tigers and the Southern League in games played (70). *Courtesy of the National Baseball Hall of Fame and Library, Cooperstown, New York.*

Batting leaders for the 1894 Nashville Tigers were first baseman Charles Dooley (.332), second baseman John O'Brien (.319) and shortstop Pete Sweeney (.278). George Borchers led the Tigers pitching staff in wins (11-14) followed by George Harper (8-3).

The 1894 Nashville Tigers (24-35) finished in sixth-place (eight total teams) in the first portion of a split season. They began the second half in first place (6-3), but the league came to a halt in July as other teams ceased operations. With teams suffering through financial problems some clubs began to sell off their best players. A few teams followed the practice while others refused to continue play.

Stallings would manage the city's last representative of the original Southern League with the Nashville Seraphs in 1895. He would have a brief playing career in the National League with Brooklyn and Philadelphia. Stallings did have a successful 13-year managerial career sprinkled between 1897 and 1920. He led the Boston Braves to the 1914 World Series championship.

The 1893 Nashville Tigers (33-60) were managed by Ted Sullivan. "Ted's Tigers," as the newspaper referred, would finish last in a 12-team league. The league realized that bigger was not necessarily better with an expanded ambition. Clubs were folding due to grim finances and Birmingham was forced to move to Pensacola. In Pensacola the team would be briefly quarantined with a yellow fever scare in their home city.

The first recorded attempt to play baseball after sunset was in Hull, Mass. in September 1880. The Northern Electric Light Co. used a system of lights on three wooden towers 100 to 300 feet apart. A baseball game commenced between the employees of two Boston department stores.

Indiana hosted the next known night games in 1883 (Ft. Wayne), August and September 1888 (Indianapolis). The minor and Negro Leagues were the first teams to play baseball in the evening. The majors followed in 1935 with their first night game in Cincinnati.

Sometime near the 1929 year, Nashville's Wilson Park hosted night baseball. The ballpark was home to the Nashville Elite Giants, a black baseball club. But, poor record keeping and little exposure to black baseball have kept details of this first night game a mystery.

The Southern Association's first night game was played in 1930 in Little Rock, Ark. While the 1894 game at Athletic Park was an exhibition, it was still the first attempt in Nashville to play at night.

Records indicate that this might have been the first night baseball game played in the South.

The 1895 Nashville Seraphs

Nashville would attempt to support professional baseball with its latest franchise in the Southern League. The 1895 Nashville Seraphs season was controversial, but not necessarily on the field. Protested games and fights with umpires were not uncommon in this era when the National Pastime was evolving.

Seraphs' games were played at Athletic Park. An ad was located in an old Nashville newspaper announcing an April exhibition game with Nashville vs. Ted Sullivan's Wild Texas Steers. Admission prices included: Ladies--Opera Grand Stand 50 cents, Smokers--Grand Stand 40 cents, Bleachers 25 cents. "Ladies accompanied by gentlemen, admitted to Grand Stand free on Fridays."

Members of the league at this time were Atlanta, Chattanooga, Evansville, Little Rock, Memphis, Mobile, Montgomery, Nashville and New Orleans. Leading Nashville was player/manager George Stallings who also managed the Nashville Tigers in the previous year.

With the Southern League records of this period limited and unavailable, research for this story will omit several players' first names. The home team continued to bat first in an inning, which was their option.

Nashville opened the season on an April afternoon at Evansville, Ind. Seraphs' fans in Nashville could receive details of the games by telegraph at the Merchants' Exchange (corner of Church and College Streets) and at the Grand Opera House (Ryman Auditorium). The Ryman was built in 1892.

Nashville lost the game, 17-10, and the *Nashville American* gave a detailed summary of the game. The following paragraph reveals the passions of the time about baseball and what lay ahead for the season:

The 1895 Nashville Seraphs won a controversial Southern League champion-ship. *Courtesy of Jeremy Jones.*

The principal feature of the game was the work of Umpire Keller. His decisions were disgusting, and gave both clubs reasonable excuse for a vast amount of kicking. The Nashville infield with the exception of Stallings seemed to be suffering from a severe case of "stage fright."

By the middle of August, Nashville trailed Evansville and Atlanta in the standings. An apparently ordinary game in Nashville against Atlanta on Aug. 10 would later be pivotal in determining the Southern League champion-ship. The Seraphs lost the game 10-9 at Athletic Park behind the pitching of their ace starter, Sammy Moran. More than 1,000 fans witnessed the poor pitching performance, but the villain of the game was, of course, the umpire.

With Nashville trailing 10-8 in their ninth inning at-bat, they scored one run. With two outs, runners were on first and second with the Seraphs' first baseman Dan Sweeney at bat. Clark was the umpire and the *Nashville American* reports on Sweeney's plate appearance:

Two strikes had been called when he hit a high foul fly toward the grand stand. Wilson got under it, but his foot slipped and he did not get his hands under it at all. Just as he went to reach for it some boy in the grounds threw a glove or a cap past his head. For this alleged interference Clark called Sweeney out. Then pandemonium reigned supreme. A howling mob went after Clark and he doubtless would have been subjected to the rough treatment which his robbing tactics had earned for him but for the interferences of a package of Chief Clack's regulars and detectives. As it was, one enthusiastic fan gave him a sound nose pulling.

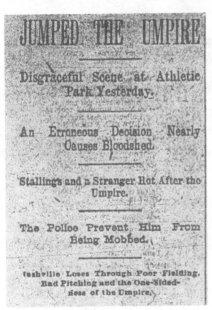

This lead to a story on a melee in August 1895 is from the Nashville American. *Courtesy of the author.*

George Wilson was Atlanta's catcher and Clack was the Nashville Chief of Police and the regulars were policemen. The game ended with a Nashville defeat, 10-9. The game would be meaningful three weeks later. With the help of a remarkable winning streak, Nashville vaulted into first place in the standings. At this time, only a few games remained on the schedule. Nashville stood at 65-35 (.650), Evansville 61-33 (.649) and Atlanta was third at 62-34 (.646).

With the teams traveling by train, games that were postponed due to rain were not rescheduled. Percentage points determined the Southern League champion. The season was scheduled to close after the games of Sept. 2. However, Atlanta won a game on Sept. 3 against New Orleans, which gave them a tie with Nashville. Nashville was 71-35 and Atlanta finished at 69-34. Nashville played three more games than Atlanta, but each team finished with the same percentage, .670.

Nashville claimed the pennant and protested the final standings due to these reasons:

They claimed that the August 10 "Glove Game" should have been thrown out due to the umpire's incorrect call. New Orleans used a player who was ineligible after he was suspended from Pennsylvania State League. Nashville insisted that the games he appeared should be forfeited. And thirdly, Atlanta played a game one day after the season was officially over and declared that the game shouldn't count in the standings.

If New Orleans were to forfeit the games in question, Nashville would be the beneficiary. The president of the Nashville team, Mr. White, gave his opinion of the controversial season ending:

"I do not think there is any necessity for talking about playing off a tie, for there is none to play off. The Nashvilles are winners of the pennant and it should be awarded to them. I would rather see that flag fly over the Nashville Base Ball Park than to be presented with a $1,000 bill as the proceeds of playing off of a tie, or from any other source.

"The action of the association may be necessary in order to officially decide the award of the pennant but of result of that action no reasonable being can have any doubt. I have only the kindest feelings for Atlanta. It is a very nice country town, and if she keeps her club together might be able some day to successfully contest with Macon and Milledgeville, Ga."

A few days later, a meeting was held in Chattanooga with the league and team representatives to determine the winner.

The American reported the results of that meeting.

The Nashville Base Ball Club of Nashville, Tenn., the club which won more games than any other club in the Southern Association and won them all fairly, not a forfeited game or an irregular game of any description being included, has justly and rightfully been declared the championship pennant winners for the season of 1895, and the pennant for which the Nashville team so earnestly fought and so fairly won by their magnificent line of twenty consecutive victories at the close of the season, will fly from the grounds of the Nashville club.

The game of Aug. 10, between Nashville and Atlanta, played at Nashville, was by unanimous vote, thrown out. This game is now the now-famous "glove game," which Clark gave to the Atlantas because some small boy in the audience threw a glove in front of Catcher Wilson while he was in the act of attempting to catch a foul ball, which he could not have

possibly reached. The ground upon which the game was thrown out was that Clark's deci-
sion was an illegal one, there being no rule providing for the punishment of a club for the
offense of an outsider.

The league also voided Atlanta's Sept. 3 game that was played after the season. With the loss taken away from the Seraph's and a win taken away from Atlanta, Nashville's percentage jumped to .676. Atlanta's percentage fell to .667. Nashville withdrew its protest of New Orleans' ineligible player.

League president, J.B. Nicklin declared the Nashville Seraphs as the 1895 Southern League champions.

The 1897 Nashville Centennials

The Southern League did not operate in 1897 therefore Nashville would join the new Central League that season.

This unidentified Nashville baseball team circa. 1900. *Courtesy of Jeremy Jones.*

The Central League's competition was much less than the Southern League. This Nashville professional baseball club was known as the Centennials named in honor of Nashville being a centennial city (Tennessee celebrated its centennial in 1896). Other league members included the Cairo (Ill) Egyptians, Evansville (Ind.) Brewers, Paducah (Ky.) Little Colonels, Terre Haute (Ind.) Hottentots and the Washington (Ind.) Browns.

The *Nashville American* reported on the upcoming needs for baseball to return to the city:

Only one thing now stands in the way of Nashville being represented in the Central League by a first-class ball team this coming season, and that is a park. The prospects are very bright for even this obstacle to be removed by refitting Athletic Park. Negotiations are in progress that bid fair to terminate satisfactorily. Billy Works is still here, and expresses himself as being very much encouraged over the outlook.

I don't know of a place in the country where I would prefer playing than Nashville," said Works during a conversation with an "American" reporter yesterday. "I learned to like the city and the people when I played here in '94, and have been anxious to get back ever since. If I succeed in getting Athletic Park put into shape for the season, I will give Nashville a team, which the people will be proud. As I have stated to you before, I have already signed three first-class men and have strings to several others that I can land any day.*

Billy Works was assigned the Nashville player/manager. He played in the outfield for the Nashville Tigers in 1894 for then-manager George Stallings. Works was asked about the Central League:

"Why, I think it a splendid one. If I wasn't confident that it would be a success, I wouldn't be willing to invest my money in a team here. I haven't got any to burn or throw away in a Fourth of July League."

A Fourth of July League is one that disbands without completing its full summer schedule. The Central League was just that. By June 2, Nashville was in first place after playing 31 games. Their 19-12 record bested second place Washington (15-10) and third place Evansville (18-13).

However the *American* gave this report in the June 3, 1897 edition with a bold caption "Outlook is Gloomy:"

The outlook for base ball in Nashville after to-day's game is somewhat gloomy. President Simon worked hard yesterday to get proper financial backing for the club, but his efforts were only partially successful. He has not entirely despaired yet, however and will renew his efforts to-day. Several gentlemen interested in the game have expressed a willingness to assist the club, and if a few more can be found to-day, the team will be a permanent institution here this summer. If no others will agree to help out the team, the team will be transferred, lock, stock and barrel to Decatur, Ill.

Some of the gentlemen who have heretofore been identified with local base ball have yet to be seen, and the fate of the team rests with them. As has been repeatedly stated in these columns, Nashville will support a team in the Central League this summer. Let the public know that the club is a permanent institution for the season and the games will be well attended. This is all that is needed, and it is to be sincerely hoped that the gentlemen interested in the great game will not permit the team to be taken away from the Centennial City for the small amount lacked to put it on a new basis.

The next day the last professional baseball game played in Nashville that year resulted in a 15-2 loss at Athletic Park to Terre Haute. The newspaper reported that the Centennials game was a "farce" since none of the local players seemed to care about playing baseball. Just before the game, the players were told the team was being transferred to Decatur.

The *American* reported on the Nashville Centennials demise with a caption that read, "Up to The Daisies, It Died a Natural Death:"

The Nashville Base Ball Club of the Central League died a natural death yesterday and, owing to the rapid decomposition of the corpse, the funeral occurred at Athletic Park in the afternoon. As was meet and proper, President Simon conducted the services and the Terre Haute team dug the grave and buried the defunct organization under an avalanche of runs. Three hundred fans were the mourners with Bob Phillips as chief. It is thought, however, that the members of the Nashville team really took the death of the club harder, deeper down in their hearts than anybody else as they had most cause for doing so.

In all seriousness, yesterday's game was the last professional base ball team that will be seen in Nashville during the year 1897. President Simon worked hard, ably and faithfully yesterday to get enough local lovers of the national game interested in the club to put it on a firm basis, but his efforts were futile and before time before yesterday's game he gave it up as a bad job.

The entire league collapsed by mid-July. However three of the Nashville Centennials players would find time in the major leagues.

Theodore Conover played for Cincinnati of the American Association in 1889. He only pitched in one game lasting two innings, giving up four hits, two walks, and one strikeout for a 13.50 ERA. The American Association was founded in 1882 and was a rival of the National League. The AA came into existence by Midwestern teams that resented the NL's ban on selling

Another unidentified Nashville baseball team circa. 1900. *Courtesy of Jeremy Jones.*

beer on Sundays. The NL absorbed most of the AA's players after the 1891 season. That league folded soon after.

Pat Dillard was an outfielder for St. Louis of the National League in 1900. He appeared in 57 games, batted .230 (42-for-183), no home runs, 12 RBI's and eight stolen bases.

Charlie Petty was born in Nashville in1866. He pitched for Cincinnati (American Association) in 1889 where he was 2-2 in five starts. Petty pitched for New York (NL) in 1893 where he was 5-2 in nine games. In 1894, Petty was with Washington (NL) and Cleveland (NL). Petty's career totals are 10-15 in 34 games with a 5.41 ERA.

Professional baseball would not return to Nashville until 1901 as members of the new Southern Association.

The 1901 Nashville "Fishermen"

When the original Southern League folded, baseball was emerging as the most popular sport with the fans. This was true in the South and especially in Nashville. The city's Athletic Park was full of baseball activity—spring through fall.

Amateur and semi-professional teams played regularly with barnstorming teams from across the country also participating. In the fall of 1900, a group of men with baseball experience met to organize a new league in the South. One of these men was native Nashvillian Newt Fisher. The 29-year-old Fisher was a minor league player with major league experience in 1898 with the Philadelphia Phillies.

The founders organized the Southern Association with 12 men on a roster and a salary cap of $1,200 per club. The average salary was $85 per player. Teams traveled by train and slept in the cheapest hotels. The original teams were Nashville, Little Rock, Memphis, New Orleans Shreveport, Chattanooga, Birmingham and Selma. A 120-game schedule would be attempted in the spring of 1901.

Though lacking an official nickname, "Fishermen" was a moniker used to refer to the Nashville club in local newspapers derived from their manager. Michael Finn replaced Fisher as manager in 1905 and the team was the "Finnites." The "Dobbers" resulted from 1907 Nashville manager Johnny Dobbs. Writing for the *Nashville Daily News* in 1901, Grantland Rice did use the unofficial name "Wanderers" for the Nashville club while on road trips.

In 1908 three local newspapers *Nashville American*, *Nashville Banner* and the *Nashville Tennessean* held a naming contest for the ball club. Grantland Rice was the *Tennessean's* editor at the time and he announced on February 29 with a bold caption: "VOLUNTEERS" THE PICK. Rice wrote:

THE VOLUNTEERS in a common canter!

By an overwhelming vote the local fan colony has picked the above as the Nashville sobriquet for all to come. The official count registered 950 votes for this nickname, while The Rocks and The Lime-Rocks were so far distanced that they were not even in the running as any stage of the contest.

Except for a few straggling votes, the bulk of the fans were decided in favor of The Volunteers—and so it will stand. The days of The Fishermen, The Finnites, The Boosters, The Dobbers, etc., are over. The name selected is one that can stand, no matter who the manager or owner may be.

"Volunteers" would last until 1963 and eventually shortened to the "Vols."

Just prior to the start of the 1901 season, league president R.W. Kent, issued a directive to all of the league's umpires. The *Nashville American* printed his instructions, which said in part:

You are absolute master of the field from the beginning to the termination of the game. I will sustain you in everything as long as you show me you are capable, industrious and honest. You need never be afraid of complaints from Presidents, managers or other persons interested in the association when you adhere strictly to the above.

In assuming control of a game, you will familiarize yourself with the batting order of each club. See that all foul lines are distinctively marked; 3-foot line and coaching lines can be plainly seen. Just before you call the game, face the grandstand and give the names of the batteries, example as follows: The battery for Shreveport to-day is Green and Jones, and for Memphis, Smith and Little.

Never in any case allow players to argue decisions with you. The Captain is the only man who has a right to address you, and it is always your duty to keep him in the limits of respectability. You have full power to fine or remove any player from the game, at any time, for infringing any way whatever on the rules. If any player continues to make trouble for you, I will handle him.

Nashville opened the regular season in Chattanooga and returned home after a three-game sweep of the Lookouts. Opening day at Athletic Park drew the attention of the city on May 6. A gala festival marked the occasion.

At 2:00 p.m., the team, led by a band, left the Duncan Hotel in carriages with Nashville Mayor James Head and other city officials. Over 2,000 fans were disappointed as their hometown club lost to Chattanooga, 9-7.

Fisher was the catcher, manager and occasionally filled in at first base. His lineup for that first Southern Association game in Nashville was: Ed Abbaticchio, second base; Doc Wiseman, right field; Fisher, first base; James Ballantyne, catcher; Lang, center field; Tom Parrott, left field; George Reitz, third base; Sherman Kennedy, shortstop; Corbett, pitcher.

By the July 4th holiday, Nashville was in second place (31-21) behind Little Rock, trailing by one game. Two games scheduled in Nashville with Birmingham revealed the seriousness to which the national pastime had evolved. The July 2nd and 3rd games with Birmingham were forfeited to Nashville, 9-0 as the Barons' manager, Sam Mills, protested the umpire.

The 1901 Nashville baseball team was a charter member of the new Southern Association that won the first league pennant. *Courtesy of the Nashville Public Library, the Nashville Room.*

Mills refused to play the games due to the presence of the umpire named York. Three days earlier, in a Nashville victory over Birmingham, Mills was upset with York's umpiring and was kicked out of the game. An unnamed reporter for the *Nashville American* explained that incident:

The Birmingham team claim that York was in error in deciding that Kennedy had stolen second in Monday's game, and that Corbett was out in the last inning for not touching second and third bases when making a circuit after his drive over the fence. From the reporter's table it could be seen that York was correct in his first decision, for the second baseman never touched Kennedy. He got the ball in time, but it was a high throw and Kennedy slid under before the ball could be brought to touch him. The latter decision, which affected the final score, was one the writer could not see, because of the crowd swarming on the field.

Mills sent a telegram to Kent requesting that York be suspended from umpiring future league games. Mills' request was denied and he was fined $100 per game for not playing. After the second forfeiture, Mills rage was apparent as he made serious accusations against York and Fisher. Fisher is quoted in the newspaper answering the Mills' outburst:

"I want you to correct some misstatements made by Mills. He states that York was drunk in Birmingham and could not umpire two games. This is not true. I saw York everyday that we were in Birmingham and he was not the least bit intoxicated. For some time prior to our going there York had been suffering with an attack of malarial fever, and that was the reason he could not officiate the two games he was out.

"I understand that Mills said that I gave York $5 while at Birmingham, implying thereby that I had bought him. I have been playing professional ball for ten years, and was never a party to a dirty transaction, and have never seen anything crooked done by any manager."

The two forfeits would later benefit Nashville as by mid-August they held a two-game lead over Memphis. All games that were postponed due to bad weather would be rescheduled whenever possible and doubleheaders were popular.

With only two weeks left until the end of the season, Little Rock was now pursuing Nashville in the hotly contested pennant race. While playing in Little Rock, more umpiring problems forced the police to become involved with fights, arrests and near-riotous fans. The *Nashville American* gave this report on that August incident:

The scheduled double-header between Little Rock and Nashville broke up in a row this afternoon and resulted in the arrest of Umpire John E. Johnstone and First Baseman Joe Wright, of the local club. Wright was bailed out within an hour, but Johnstone was refused bail until to-night on account of the fear of danger to him from the excited populace which surrounded the jail to the number of 500.

The problem that led to the ruckus was the issue of who was to umpire the game and the eligibility of a Nashville pitcher. Nashville brought Johnstone with them on the train to Little Rock while the normal Little Rock umpire was James Murray. Murray would not relinquish the field to Johnstone. When Nashville refused to play the game without Johnstone as the umpire, Murray forfeited the game to Little Rock.

Documentation finally appeared form the league's president that Johnstone was scheduled to umpire the game. Another issue that riled Little Rock was the pitcher for Nashville, Bailey, who recently joined Nashville. Bailey had previously pitched with Selma, but was traded to Nashville the day before. Another telegram from the league president confirmed Bailey's status with Nashville. The Arkansans were not satisfied with either ruling. The *Nashville American* continued their story of the controversy during this heated pennant race:

> *Little Rock took the field in the first inning, with Popp pitching, and Nashville made two runs. When Little Rock went to bat, Bailey walked to the box over Little Rock's protest. Crozier, of Little Rock, was on second when Martin singled and Crozier attempted to score. The ball got to the plate just as Crozier did, and Catcher Fisher, swung at him and apparently missed him, but the umpire called Crozier out.*
>
> *First Baseman Wright, who was sitting on the bench, ran into the diamond and, pushing against Johnstone, knocked him down. When Johnstone got up it is alleged he attempted to strike Wright. Policemen ran to the diamond and placed Johnstone under arrest. Wright was also arrested, and both were taken to city jail.*
>
> *Nashville refused to continue the game unless Johnstone umpired.*

The mayor of Little Rock was in attendance and spoke before the 5,000 fans. He stated it was best to send Wright and Johnstone to city jail. It was reported that Nashville exited the field and later they were ordered to forfeit the game to Little Rock.

Nashville shortstop Willis Butler chokes up on the bat in a game in Nashville's Athletic Park (Sulphur Dell) in 1908. *Courtesy of the National Baseball Hall of Fame and Library, Cooperstown, New York.*

In a public relations maneuver, Fisher fired off a telegram to the *Nashville American* to relate his side of the story. The telegram was printed at the end of the newspaper's story of the entire incident. Fisher's telegram:

"Our treatment here by the police, city officials and the Little Rock club has been something awful from the moment of our arrival. The games to-day broke up in a riot. Wright assaulted Johnstone during the game and knocked him down. The police first arrested, Johnstone then Wright, The trouble was anticipated, as the patrol wagon was on the grounds. The manager refused to let the game continue. Wright was intoxicated. We will get both games."

A determined and emotional Fisher followed his telegram with a second that was also published for Nashville's consumption:

"Press reports say that I took my team from the field and that Johnstone assaulted the Little Rock player. That is false. Wright was intoxicated and assaulted Johnstone during the game. It was a deliberate conspiracy on the part of the officials and people to rob us. I was prepared for them. I have just seen the operator who sent out the false report. My boys kicked him out of the hotel. Johnstone gives Nashville both games. Johnstone was not only knocked down, but kicked also. I am right and will stick up for my end."

The Vols did hold on to claim the pennant despite some controversial encounters throughout the year. No team in the league was fully satisfied with the umpires. When all the season's protests and records were sorted out, Nashville (78-45) was declared the inaugural champs of the Southern Association by four games.

Pitcher Warren Sanders (21-9) led the team in wins while Ed Abbaticchio led Nashville in batting (.360) and the league in runs scored (127).

The 1902 Nashville Baseball Club

Nashville, Tennessee was the home of the Southern Association's first defending champions as the league entered its second season in 1902. The "Fishermen" hoisted its championship pennant of the previous season at Athletic Park after a nine-game, season-opening road trip.

A rare championship in Nashville from a professional team was cause for a parade along the prominent streets of the city. The "Gray and Dudley Band" led the 1902 edition of the Nashville ball club to the ballpark for its 4:00 p.m. game. Following closely behind in a carriage was Nashville Mayor James Head, President Garrabrant of the Retail Merchants Association and President Palmer of the Capital City Base Ball & Athletic Association.

Just prior to the home opener against Birmingham in front of 3,000 fans, Head approached the pitching mound to toss the ceremonial first pitch to Palmer. At that same moment of the ceremonial first pitch, the 1901 championship banner rose above the flagpole located on "the Summer Street dump in the rear of centerfield," a newspaper stated.

Player/manager Newt Fisher led his Nashville club to a 10-3 victory.

Optimism was high for the season, as most of the previous championship team was intact. The umpire was usually someone living in a league member city and umpired that city's home games. This meant more controversial calls and accusations, especially for the visiting clubs.

Nashville baseball fans could follow the team on the road for special excursion prices. A round trip train fare from the Nashville rail station to Memphis would cost a Vols' fan only $3.50. Fans not able to make a trip could gather at certain downtown venues such as lodges, theaters or bowling alleys for

The 1902 Nashville baseball team won the city's second consecutive Southern Association championship with player/manager Newt Fisher. *Courtesy of the Metropolitan Government Archives of Nashville and Davidson County.*

telegraph or telephone updates. Tickets could be purchased at downtown hotels or at Athletic Park. Oh yes, the telephone number for the ballpark in 1902 was—1957.

Other members of the association at this time were New Orleans, Chattanooga, Little Rock, Atlanta, Memphis, Birmingham and Shreveport. At the end of May, Nashville was in first place at 18-7, just one game ahead of New Orleans. One particular May afternoon game in Nashville against Memphis revealed the financial importance of rain delays and rainouts. The *Nashville American* gave this report:

Umpire Strauss announced to the spectators, a large number who were ladies, that under the laws and constitution governing the organization, he was not allowed to call the game while it was raining, and that he would wait fifteen minutes, the time specified in the laws, and if by that time the weather did not change he would have to call the game off.

Fifteen minutes later, Strauss did go by the rules and announced to the grandstand that the game was postponed. He also announced that rain checks would be given at the box office or for those wanting refund of their quarters, should also visit the box office. A mob gathered at the gate for their refunds, which wasn't necessarily the rule of that day. The *American* continued:

Strauss made a mistake in announcing that money would be refunded to those desiring, as it is not customary for the coin to be returned when a game is called on the account of rain. The man at the box office refused to "come across," and there was a howl from some of the spectators. Fisher and Frank were consulted, but they would not consent to return the money at first. On learning, however, that a number of those present were visitors, being in Nashville to attend the State Democratic Convention, the moguls cheerfully ordered the ticket seller to give the money back that wished it.

Memphis manager Charley Frank will become the major story of the Southern Association that season. While on July 8th the Vols had secured first place in the standings at 42-13 and a six-game lead over New Orleans. Accusations of "contract jumping" hit the Memphis team.

Memphis pitcher, Jim St. Vrain, had been under contract with Tacoma, Wash., the previous season, but joined Memphis. The National Association of Minor League Clubs suspended Frank for ten days and fined him $100. Two other Memphis players, Charlie Babb and William Evans, were being investigated for the same offense. But Frank disregarded the suspensions.

All games in which St. Vrain had participated were declared a forfeit. However, a stubborn Frank refused to abide by the rulings, as St. Vrain's next start was in Nashville. St. Vrain did start the game and got the victory. Memphis brought an attorney to Nashville and would have filed an injunction if Fisher refused to play the game.

As more pressure was put on Frank from the league and National Association of National Leagues, the manager declared St. Vrain "ill" in his next start at home against the Vols. Some bad feelings around the league were aimed at Fisher for failing to follow league instructions not to play Memphis with ineligible players.

The NANL secretary, Farrell, told Finn, the Little Rock official, to organize the other league members to find a replacement for the Memphis

This 1902 Nashville team photo was taken in New Orleans during a series with the Pelicans. *Courtesy of the National Baseball Hall of Fame and Library, Cooperstown, New York.*

team. There was a threat that if action was not taken against Frank and the Memphis team, the Southern Association could be expelled from their organization. The *American* published Finn's frustration:

"I don't think the Southern League can afford to dally in this matter any longer," said Finn to the writer yesterday. "If the Southern League expected to exist only a month or so we might disregard Ferrell's threats, but as the Southern League expects to operate for several seasons, yet we are necessarily compelled to do what Ferrell tells us to."

"I can understand readily why Manager Fisher might be willing to do all in his power to help Frank, without directly infringing the base ball laws, and I do not blame Mr. Fisher. He and Frank have been friends for years and Fisher would naturally like to give his friend all the support possible that can be at all consistent with base ball law. But there are six other clubs in this league to be considered and I can say these six are a unit against Frank's policy in retaining St. Vrain in opposition to secretary Ferrell's orders.

"The principal trouble with this league is that it hasn't got a president with a backbone. I told President Nicklin that Frank seemed to be bossing the league at present, and it looks to me that this is really the case."

The league officials met the next day (July 19) and decided to fine any league member $100 for playing in a game with Frank or St. Vrain. Memphis and all the league teams were telegrammed with their rulings. However, the officials were slapped with an injunction by Memphis attorneys "from taking any action or making any orders or doing anything impeding or hindering the rights of the Memphis Base Ball Club to continue to play in the Southern Association of Base Ball Clubs, and with the clubs constituting the same, and that each and every member of the directory be restrained from expelling or attempting to expel or enforcing or promulgating and order or act of forfeiture or expulsion."

With tensions mounting within the league, a defiant Frank scheduled St. Vrain to pitch the very next day after the injunction. The site of this game, which had the eyes of southern baseball enthusiasts watching closely, was once again in Nashville. Frank, backed by the injunction, watched Nashville beat his controversial pitcher, 6-0.

By the middle of August, the league was fed up with their situation. There were rumors of trial dates and out of court settlements. The league once again met and decided to take a tougher stand against Memphis and their attorneys. The officials instructed any team that played a game in which Frank or St. Vrain was involved; the umpire was instructed to forfeit the game to their opponent, 9-0. Failure to obey this directive would be grounds for the umpire's dismissal.

Attorney's for the Memphis Club immediately filed a suit against the league for $10,000 in damages to the Memphis club. In his frustration over the entire situation, J. B. Nicklin resigned as president of the league. A few weeks later, the new president,

These individual photos of the 1902 Nashville players were published in a 1903 spring issue of the Sporting News. *Courtesy of the National Baseball Hall of Fame and Library, Cooperstown, New York.*

William M. Kavanaugh, instructed Nashville not to play any more games since St. Vrain and Frank were involved in Memphis' last trip of the season to Athletic Park. Fisher responded to the directive.

"What am I to do?" asked Fisher when asked if he would play with St. Vrain in the frame. "Mr. Tyne, the Nashville club's attorney, advises me to allow St. Vrain to play. Frank swears that he will have me arrested for contempt of court if I refuse to play the game, and then here is over half the crowd clamoring for a game, no matter who pitches or who doesn't pitch. If I refuse to play I will do so contrary to my lawyer's opinion and advice.

"A majority of the people who pay their money to see ball played care little for these controversies, except in an abstract sort of way. They want to see a game, no matter who pitches, and I believe that I am pleasing the greater portion of base ball patrons in playing the game, and at the same time I am following the advice of my lawyer and the dictates of common sense."

Kavanaugh backed downed and rescinded his order that Nashville was to suspend play. He cited the injunction against the league for his latest actions. Could this baseball season be anymore confusing?

The season finally ended with Nashville (82-42) winning the pennant for the second straight season. The Vols won by six games as the season concluded with the conflict not resolved.

The *American* published a story to concerning the confusion:

There is but one person in all base ball that kept a record of the result of games as actually played in the Southern League with no attention paid to the various forfeitures and complications which were caused by the row over St. Vrain, says the Memphis Commercial Appeal. That person was editor Richter, of the Philadelphia Sporting Life. According to his record Nashville won the pennant by a wider margin in 1901, and New Orleans finished in second place.

The *American* gave its opinion:

The Nashville base ball team has won the pennant fairly and squarely by playing a steadier and more consistent game than any other team. The club began the season on equal terms and each one had an equal chance to land the first prize.

The pennant has been won on its merits and the fans of this city should show their appreciation when the boys "come marching home."

In the fall the cases against the league and Memphis were resolved out of court. After the suspensions, forfeits and reverse forfeits were sorted out Nashville was the official winner.

Lost in the turmoil of the season was the .416 league leading batting average by Vols' outfielder Hugh Hill. The spectacular hitting performance would establish a Southern Association record that was never broken. However, his average has been challenged in recent years. Hill also doubled as a pitcher, posting a 22-7 record.

Greatest Baseball Game Played in the South

If you have ever used the parking lot (now the location of First Tennessee Park) located on the 800 block of Fourth Ave. North, you were parked over a once-sacred plot. Beneath the pavement was the soil that once was trampled on by Cap Anson, Cy Young, Babe Ruth, Honus Wagner, Ted Williams, Joe DiMaggio, Jackie Robinson, Henry Aaron and many other baseball legends. This was the location of the Sulphur Dell ballpark, home of the Nashville Vols baseball club. It is also the historic site of what newspapers across the country proclaimed as "The greatest baseball game ever played in the South."

The Vols entered the game with an identical 56 losses with the New Orleans Pelicans. But, the Pelicans were in first place with 76 wins versus 74 for the second-place Vols.

At stake was the Southern Association pennant since this was the final game of the season. Postponed games were not rescheduled at this late stage of the season. It was a winner-take-all with percentage points determining the champion.

Oh yes, this was the greatest game ever played in the South, that is, up until 1908.

The Vols had won the pennant in 1901 and 1902, the first two seasons of the newly formed Southern Association. This game was played on Sunday, Sept. 19, 1908. Anticipation was at the highest level for this game. Stores near the ballpark had to close since their male employees would not work and left for the game.

Over 11,000 fans overflowed the ballpark, which was the largest attendance for a baseball game in the South. The grandstand and bleachers were

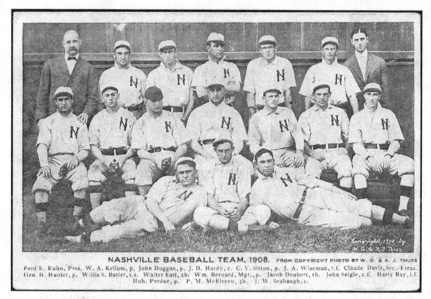

NASHVILLE BASEBALL TEAM, 1908. FROM COPYRIGHT PHOTO BY W. G. & A. J. THUSS
Ferd E. Kuhn, Pres. W. A. Kellum, p. John Duggan, p. J. D. Hardy, c. C. V. Sitton, p. J. A. Wiseman, r.f. Claude Davis, Sec.-Treas.
Geo. H. Hunter, p. Willis S. Butler, s.s. Walter East, 2b. Wm. Bernard, Mgr., p. Jacob Daubert, 1b. John Seigle, c.f. Harry Bay, l.f.
Hub. Perdue, p. P. M. McElveen, 3b. J. W. Seabaugh, c.

The 1908 Nashville baseball team is displayed in this vintage post card. *Courtesy of Jeremy Jones.*

swarming as the crowd began to gather three hours before the afternoon start. Seats were borrowed from Vanderbilt University, and they were soon filled when assembled.

The spectators eventually stretched around the outfield, lining under the fence in right and center. Hundreds of people stood on the nearby railroad tracks behind leftfielder. Including the "slip-ins," a conservative crowd estimate rose to 12,500 by game time.

Grantland Rice wrote in *The Tennessean* about the hometown Vols and their pending historic day.

There were no individual brilliant stars on the Volunteer line-up. There was not a .300 hitter in the entire squad. But man for man they matched every other team in the league. A large majority of the boys batted around .265 to .288. It was this high average made them formidable. While there was no great star among them, there was not an inferior among them. They ranked high as hard-working, consistent, capable men, and their team, work made them invincible.

Nashville player/manager Bill Bernhard gave the ball to 26-year-old pitcher Vedder Sitton. The Pelicans countered with 39-year-old veteran

Theodore Breitenstein who had 11 years of major league experience, but wandered in the minors since 1902. It was a David vs. Goliath billing.

The fans were not disappointed as the expected pitching duel began with Sitton striking out the first batter of the game. The bout was scoreless through six innings while Sitton gave up two hits in the second and fourth innings. Breitenstein gave up a hit in the Vols' half of the first with two additional Vols' hits occurring in the 4th inning.

First baseman Jake Daubert led off the home side of the seventh, popping out to the shortstop with Kid Butler following with a ground out to first. The next batter, catcher Ed Hurlburt, stroked a sharp single to right field. Sitton punched a roller to Pelicans first baseman Bob Tarleton, who botched a bare-hand pickup, resulting in an infield hit for the Vols' pitcher. Harry "Deerfoot" Bay dropped a surprise bunt just barely beating out the throw to first. The bases were jammed with two outs with rightfielder Doc Wiseman the next batter.

Wiseman connected on the Breitenstein's pitch, slapping the ball over the second baseman's out-reached glove. Hurlburt scored from third while Sitton, trying to score from second, was called for the third out at the plate due to a perfect throw from New Orleans centerfielder Bris Lord.

During Sitton's slide at the plate, he hit the back of his head on the catcher's knee. Sitton staggered to the dugout and nearly collapsed into his teammates arms. Bernhard did not have any intentions on leaving Sitton in the game. Sitton broke loose from his teammates, who tried to keep him on the bench, but took his place on the mound.

When Wiseman jogged to his right field position, the elated outfield fans approached him, and the police were hustled onto the field to push the fans back into their section. After Johnny Matthews fanned to began the Pelicans' eighth, the masses began screaming, "Sitton! Sitton! Sitton!" He retired the side while the Vols went out in their half of the eighth.

In the top of the ninth, Pelicans leadoff batter Thomas Rohe grounded out to Vols' second sacker Walter East for the first out. The 11,000-plus Nashvillians jumped to their feet and once again began chanting, "Sitton! Sitton! Sitton!"

Vedder Sitton was the winning pitcher for Nashville that won the 1908 Southern Association championship on the final day of the season. *Courtesy of the National Baseball Hall of Fame and Library, Cooperstown, New York.*

Sitton struck out the final two batters, recording a total of nine strikeouts and three hits. The Nashville Vols won the 1908 Southern Association pennant as reported in *The Tennessean*:

The greatest pennant race that any league has ever known was decided here this afternoon when the Nashville Volunteers won from the New Orleans Pelicans, winning the game 1-0, and the Southern League championship by one point.

The game was witnessed by the largest crowd that has seen a ball game in any southern city this season. There were 10,400 paid admissions and hundreds saw the game from the tops of fences, trees and every possible point of vantage.

This was the first time in the history of organized baseball that a championship hinged on one game played between the two leading teams. It was the first time in baseball history that a championship was won by one point and by one run--in this case, the only run in the game.

Nashville wins the championship with a percentage of .572; New Orleans finished with .571. The Vols, won the game clearly. Though if the Pelicans had played perfect ball or even up to their form on the road trip the score would possibly have been reversed.

As the third strike was called to end the game, thousands of fans swarmed towards the exhausted Sitton while he was embracing his teammates. Six policemen raced to the aid of Sitton, but were themselves swept away by the army of fans. Sitton struggled to leave the field. In desperation he, "reached for a copper's billy to keep the crowd away," the *Tennessean* reported.

The exuberant fans eventually overwhelmed him, as they lifted him into the air. Women tried to kiss him and hundreds tried to shake his hand at the same time. The wiring and planks would not detain the hordes in the grandstand when they broke through the lumber and anything in their way. An estimated several hundred dollars of damage was placed on the ball park.

It was an inspiring spectacle when Sitton struck out the last two men in the ninth and ended the game. The thousands in the grandstand and on the bleachers stood and yelled themselves hoarse, while the other thousands surrounding the field surged upon the diamond and carried the victorious Volunteers aloft on their shoulders.

The players made a break to get off the field, but the captured them and almost mobbed them in their delight. The whole diamond and field were literally packed with shouting, frenzied, hilariously maddened throng. It was a great climax to one of the greatest diamond battles ever fought out in the south.

Not a demonstration of violence was made. Every man, woman and child cheered and cheered hard for their home team, and there was not a minute that old Sulphur Dell was not ringing with the voices of the thousands, and the bells, horns and artificial contrivances of the craziest ball bugs on the continent.

The demonstration lasted for nearly 30 minutes, as men tossed their hats into the air and everybody "singing songs of victory." The president of the Nashville Boosters, Iser Peter Cohen, realized the city would benefit from the publicity of the championship. Mr. Cohen advised the Vols management that he would present four of his famous "Petersee" brand of dress shirts to each member of the team.

Sitton received $100.00 from adoring fans for his pitching achievement. He was mobbed in downtown Nashville as he walked the streets that night after the game. Wiseman, who had been a fan favorite all season, received a gold watch valued at $175 while the members of the Watauga Club donated $50 to their hero, also showing their appreciation.

Newspapers in all portions of the United States requested copies of the stories printed by the Nashville newspapers. Requests also came from the *Associated Press* and the *Hearst News Service* keeping the city's sportswriters working overtime. Telegrams of congratulations poured in from all over the country from politicians and baseball administrators.

Nashville's own Grantland Rice wrote of the game in his unique and elegant style.

Facing a veteran who had grown old in service--a veteran who had reached the end of the greatest season he had ever known, with one more fight to win -- the blonde-haired Volunteer loomed up as the spectacular figure of the matinee.

Bill Bernhard was a player/manager for Nashville from 1908-1910. *Courtesy of the National Baseball Hall of Fame and Library, Cooperstown, New York.*

Surrounded by 11,000 people whom he knew were watching every turn and twist he made, the youngster entered the ring with his veteran rival as confident of the outcome as if sundown had already proclaimed him victor.

There was never a quiver that told of nervousness--never a faller that told of a weakening stride--never a let-up in an attack that fairly hammered Frank's people into a shapeless mass-- but, coming on with a rush that grew stronger and stronger round by round until at the windup the dazed Birds were walloping the empty air with no apparent idea of where the ball happened to be just at that particular moment.

The 1908 edition of the championship Nashville Vols gained so much attention that the major leagues ascended upon the city to swipe their players. The St. Louis Browns signed Kid Butler, Cleveland landed Jake Daubert, Harry Bay and Vedder Sitton. Brooklyn also grabbed from Nashville, Humpy McElveen and pitcher George Hunter while pitcher Johnny Duggan was picked up by Pittsburgh. The now-depleted Nashville Vols would not win another pennant until 1916.

So, the next time you are standing on this Fourth Avenue North site, listen for those faint screams of "Sitton! Sitton! Sitton!" by your Nashville ancestral spirits. Now you will know what the shouting was about.

Sunday Baseball Banned in 1911

In the late 19th century, many frowned upon playing baseball on a Sunday. The Sabbath was supposed to be set-aside for a day of rest. From time to time a community would resist Sunday baseball by taking legal action in the courts. Such was a case in Nashville with a 1911 game between the hometown Vols and New Orleans Pelicans at Sulphur Dell. The Saturday May 27, 1911 edition of the *Nashville Tennessean* gave a preview of what was to come:

"Determined that the baseball game scheduled between Nashville and New Orleans for Sunday afternoon shall not be played if the provisions of the law will prevent it, the Men's Christian Union became busy yesterday and members of the union after the days work expressed complete confidence that with co-operation on the part of the city and county officials the participants, if the game is commenced, will be arrested and rearrested as often as the effort is made to play. Another meeting of the union and citizens interested in the enforcement of the law preventing the game will be held this morning at 11 o'clock at the First Presbyterian Church.

"So again the question is up as to whether the game will be carried out and then published statutes of the law violated. Those protesting against the game state that arrangements are made for the arrests not only of the captains of the teams, but all participating, and not only once but as often as the effort is made to resume the game. Magistrates and constables will be on the grounds and everything will be in readiness they say.

"Sheriff Borum said last night: 'No matter what my personal feelings may be in the case, if warrants are placed in my hands, of course I will serve them. I can have no discretion in the matter, and whatever I have been accused of,

I don't believe the question of my duty to the warrants placed in my hands has been or need question.

"As soon as it became rumored that Managers Schwartz of Nashville and Frank of New Orleans had scheduled the Sunday game the union commenced the same tactics pursued recently when plans had been made for the Nashville-Atlanta Sunday game and at the meeting yesterday morning appointed a committee of fifteen to see the officials, asking that the law he enforced and the game prevented. The committee named was: Dr. G. C. Savage, chairman; Dr. Allen G. Hall, I. L. Pendleton, J. W. Hunter, Jr., J. D. Blanton, E. R. Richardson, Leland Hume, J. L. Watts, John A. Pitts, Dr. McPheeters Glasgow, Dr. W. C. Gillespie, A. Tillman Jones, M. G. Buckner, F. J. Ehrhart and C. T. Cheek.

"Manager Frank arrived in Nashville yesterday afternoon and told a reporter that he was here not to dictate in the matter, but to do whatever was decided on locally. 'I am in the hands of the local baseball association,' he said, 'and aren't ready to follow out their orders, play or not play.'"

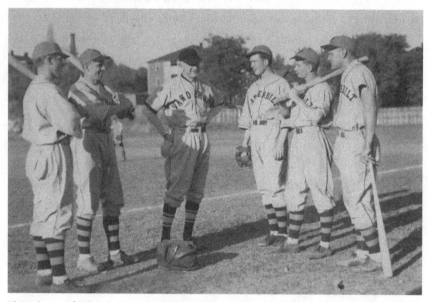

This photo of Bill Schwartz (center) is from 1938 as the Vanderbilt head baseball coach (1917, 1924-40) He also managed the Vols (1911-14). *Courtesy of Vanderbilt University Special Collections and Archives.*

The game was played, but with several interruptions throughout the contest. The Vols lost the nine-inning game, 10-8. The Monday, May 29, 1911 edition of *the Nashville Tennessean* reported on Sunday's events:

"A game of professional baseball was played in Nashville yesterday for the first time in more than 25 years. Twenty-three arrests were made. Those on whom papers were served will appear before Justice J. O. Gaffney at 10 o'clock this morning. W. G. Hirsig, president of the local ball club, and William C. Schwartz, manager, were arrested shortly after the game began by a municipal warrant served by city detectives B. T. Cummins and W. E. Jacobs, and charged with playing a game of ball on Sunday. Between the third and fourth innings eight arrests of the players on bench warrants sworn out by Dr. M. G. Buckner and Dr. J. D. Blanton before A. B. Tavel and Jesse Cage, magistrates, in an automobile just outside the grounds, were made by Sheriff Sam H. Borum and Constable William Cockrell, the latter serving two warrants. Between the fifth and sixth inning Constable William Cockrell served thirteen bench warrants upon thirteen players.

"In each instance those named in the warrant appeared before the officer, acknowledged arrest and an appearance bond of $250 was made by President Hirsig before Judge Gaffney who was called to the field each time from the grandstand, with the exception of the municipal arrest of President Hirsig and Manager Schwartz, who were informed by City Detective Jacobs that they might appear immediately after the game at the police station and arrange for bond.

"The game started promptly at 3:30 o'clock, shortly afterward a large automobile containing Dr. Buckner, Mr. Blanton, G. S. Moore, Justice Tavel, J. L. Pendleton and I. Cockrell of the Men's Christian Union, stopped at the main entrance to Athletic Park. Justice Cage arrived shortly afterwards. Dr. Buckner and Dr. Blanton then swore out bench warrants for William Schwartz, Doc Wiseman, Juan Viola, Harry Bay, Red Smith, Henry Keupper of the Nashville club, and Umpires Fitzsimmions and Colliflower. One of these warrants was given to Deputy Sheriff Joseph Ezell and the remainder taken to Sheriff Borum at the entrance.

"A controversy ensued between Sheriff Borum, Deputy Ezell and members of the Men's Christian Union party, the sheriff claiming that Deputy Ezell was only commissioned for the purpose of collecting for a collection agency and not for making criminal arrests. Deputy Ezell claimed that his commission did not state that and he has sworn to uphold law and order.

"Sheriff Borum stated that he brought with him eighteen deputy sheriffs commissioned for criminal arrests and asked Deputy Ezell to turn in his commission today, to which the latter asserted. When the sheriff and several of his deputies served the warrants there were hisses from some of the spectators.

"Constable William Cockrell was given the next warrants to serve on the following players: Harry Bay, Doc Wiseman, Warren Seabough, Teddy Bair and William Bordeiser, of the Nashville Club, Umpires Fitzsimmons and Colliflower, and Johnston, Kirke, Callahan, Doane, Frazer and Veasey of the New Orleans Club.

"The following volunteered to accompany Constable Cockrell and aid him, if necessary, in arresting and removing the players from the field: R. C. Reeves, P.W. Cavender, J. Boiling, Harry Hughes, Henry Jordan, Joseph Ezell, H. A. Myers and Dr. Blanton. The party was unable to get through the gates, and at the manager's office only constable Cockrell was permitted inside the grandstand. A semi-scuffle ensued at the doorway, the crowd, in the rear striving to push those forward into the grandstand.

"The service of the warrants culminated, as did former service, the players being called from the field at the end of the inning, acknowledging service and Mr. Hirsig making bond before Justice Gaffney. The action of the officers in permitting bond to be made on the grounds and the game to continue was much decried by the members of the committee from the Men's Christian Union."

Dr. Blanton, of the Men's Christian Union, was not pleased that bonds could be made on the stadium site or the next day and the game continued. He was also upset that Sheriff Borum did not support Deputy Ezell by taking the men served with warrants to the police station for processing. Dr. Blanton made the following statement:

"I think it is an outrage when a city comes to the pass when you can only find two officers who are willing to issue warrants with a view of breaking up a baseball game which is in violation of the law. And when the sheriff finds one of these is his deputy he at once revokes his commission. We have reached a period of anarchy, and it is conversely shown."

In connection with his action in revoking the commission of Deputy Ezell, Sheriff Borum made the following statement:

"I consider that I am in a measure insulted by several men whom I understand to be representatives of the Men's Christian Union. I told a committee of gentleman from that body Saturday I would be present at the ball game with all the deputies necessary to execute provisions of the law. They told me that was perfectly satisfactory, and were pleased with my decision. They agreed to meet me at the box office today and deliver the warrants in person.

"When they met me they were with a constable and a man bearing my commission to do special work, such as collecting for collection agencies. It appears to me by that action that they did not have the confidence in me that was displayed Saturday. I still stand ready to serve and execute any warrants given to me."

Outfielder Harry Bay played four seasons (1908-11) for the Nashville Vols. *Courtesy of Jeremy Jones.*

One week later, Nashville was scheduled to play Birmingham on Sunday June 4. And once again everybody showed up to play a game including the Men's Christian Union and the Sheriff's department. The *Tennessean* reported on that second Sunday game in which Birmingham defeated the Vols, 5-4:

"Despite 176 bench warrants issued by members of the Men's Christian Union a game of professional baseball was played in the city yesterday afternoon between the Nashville and Birmingham clubs. This is the second Sunday game played here for the past twenty-eight years, the first being played the previous Sunday. The warrants were served upon twenty-seven participates included players, umpire, gatekeepers and ticket sellers by Sheriff Borum and his deputies.

"Bonds in the sum of $250 each were signed by W. G. Hirsig, president the Nashville club, immediately after each service before Justice of the Peace John Gaffney. Manager William Schwartz, of the Nashville club was arrested on the municipal warrant at the close of the game.

"Warrants were served at the beginning and in the middle of each inning, eighteen services being made during the game, which was only slightly interfered with the warrants not being served until the men came in from the field."

Baseball was not played on Sundays in Nashville for the rest of the year. Sunday baseball was resumed later, but in 1916, another lawsuit was served on the Nashville Vols for playing baseball on Sunday. In that case, Sunday baseball in Nashville was stopped until 1919 after the Tennessee Supreme Court ruled for the Christian groups opposing games on the Sabbath. The Tennessee Court of Appeals overturned the Supreme Court ruling Sunday Baseball was not a violation of any law.

The Vols finished the season in fourth place with a 69-64 record and managed by Bill Schwartz.

PART II

Great Players, Great Teams, Great Events

Tom Rogers' Perfect Game in 1916

The Nashville Vols had a rich history as a major contributor to the National Pastime. In a three-week period in 1916, one of the Vols' players was involved in two separate incidents, which placed him in the baseball history books. Both were rare for a baseball game, with one becoming a career highlight and the other a tragedy.

On July 11, 1916, Vols' pitcher Tom Rogers hurled a no-hit, no-run, perfect game in Nashville's Sulphur Dell. The right-hander was born in Sparta, Tenn., in 1892, and was known as the "Gallatin Gunner." The previous season he nearly signed a contract with the St. Louis Browns, but they decided he needed more polishing at Nashville.

The Vols were in a battle with the New Orleans Pelicans for the Southern Association pennant, leading the standings by one game as this historic day began. Vols' skipper, Roy Ellam, was in a dilemma with his pitching staff shaken up by injuries and recent poor performances. Rogers was placed into the lineup with only two days rest.

The third-place Chattanooga Lookouts were in the Dell on this summer afternoon seven games behind the league-leading Vols. The Lookouts countered with left-hander Jim Allen on the mound. Allen was nearly as effective as he only allowed one hit, two walks and a hit batter in the game. The game was scoreless and hitless until a breakdown by the Chattanooga defense occurred in the 7th inning.

Vols' second baseman Tommy Sheehan led off the 7th inning with a hit to deep short for the first and only hit of the game for either team. Howard Baker sacrificed Sheehan to second, followed by a fly ball to Lookouts' centerfielder Bob Messenger. Messenger was about to make the catch when

The 1916 Nashville Vols, led by player-manager Roy Ellam, won their Southern Association championship. *Courtesy of the National Baseball Hall of Fame and Library, Cooperstown, New York.*

Lookout leftfielder Joe Harris leaped in front of Messenger, interfering with the catch. The baseball fell to the ground for an error with runners now on second and third with one out.

Vols' first baseman Dick Kauffman dropped a bunt at Allen, who bobbled the ball, scoring Sheehan from third on another error. Williams then concluded the scoring when Art Kores successfully executed a squeeze play. Roy Ellam walked and Gabby Smith popped out to finish the inning.

With two outs in the Lookout ninth, reserve catcher John Peters entered the game to pinch-hit for Allen. Not wanting his team to end the game without a hit a determined Peters hit a weak fly, which Sheehan caught for a 2-0 win.

Rogers faced 27 batters and retired each for the Vols only perfect game of their history. After the sixth inning the coaches for the Lookouts became so frustrated with Rogers' perfection, they put on a heckling show from the coaches boxes. In an attempt to upset Rogers' composure, the Lookouts began a barrage of distracting catcalls and jeering, but to no avail, as Rogers continued to mow them down.

The perfect game was in jeopardy with two smashes by the Lookouts, which resulted in great defensive catches. In the second inning, leadoff batter Harris stroked a bullet to the famous right centerfield "dump." Centerfielder Billy Lee raced toward the ball with the crack of the bat. He dove at the foot of the hill, clutching the ball as he fell forward, burying his face into the grass. The fans stormed to their feet with the exciting catch.

In the seventh, the fans were very much aware of the situation and the tensions were growing with each pitch. The perfect game was almost spoiled until another unbelievable defensive play by the Vols saved the hitless streak. This description appeared in the *Tennessean*.

To match the stunning performance Gus Williams made a seemingly impossible stab against the colored grand stand in the seventh frame off Jake Pitler. The Chattanooga second-sacker laced a pill on a dead line to left straight as an arrow towards the negro shady stands. Gus was set far towards center, but with a herculean gallop he raced under the streaking ball, snagged it as it neared the stand and crashed into the bleacher fence, swept forward with the momentum of his rapid pace.

The headlines of the newspaper prominently covered the gem with a large photo of Rogers indicating a heroic performance.

Thomas "Shotgun" Rogers climbed yesterday to the proudest pinnacle in the baseball world. The Gallatin Gunner, in the most gallant exhibition of slab work ever unfurled in this section of the more or less United States, reported with that fondly cherished dream of every gent who makes the diamond his habitat--a perfect game. One unmarred by either a run, a hit or a hostile son of swat reaching the initial corner.

In a word, the climax of twirling cunning. Like the steady sweep of a giant blade, the Gallatin Gunner's superb pitching mowed down the twenty-seven hostile Lookouts as rapidly as they came to bat. In rare rotation, without exception, the Elberfeld clan were moved into the morgue in every frame of the matchless performance.

Nothing that remotely resembled a hit could the laboring Lookouts prize from the cunning of the Gunner's whip. Not a bobble did his mates contribute behind him. Not a free pass did he give out. Not a batter did he hit and for nine brilliant and bizarre rounds three Lookouts were retired in the order of their appearance at the plate.

Only twice did a Lookout bid for a safe smash. Joe Harris and Jake Pitler erupted a smash a piece that was ticketed to shatter the dream of Shotgun Rogers. The Brace of the Lookouts larrupers smote the ball with all the fervor of a pile driver. Yet Billy Lee and Gus Williams turned the wallops into deaths with two of the most astonishing catches that have ever been exhibited in any man's ball yard.

Just three weeks earlier, Rogers was involved with one of the rarest tragedies that can occur in baseball. A Rogers' pitch struck Mobile (Ala.) Gulls' batter Johnny Dodge in the face on June 18, 1916, in Mobile, Ala. He was knocked unconscious and died the next day. Dodge was born in Bolivar, Tenn., and a former Vols' teammate of Rogers the previous season.

Nashville pitcher Tom Rogers tossed a perfect game on July 11, 1916 at Sulphur Dell against Chattanooga. Courtesy of the *National Baseball Hall of Fame and Library*, Cooperstown, New York.

The 23-year-old Dodge gained major league experience with the Phillies and the Reds in 1912-13. The infielder's limited ability produced a career .215 average, which sent him back into the minors.

The newspaper regrettably reported Dodge's death:

The Great Umpire has called Johnny out. There will be no more "close plays" for the former Vol in that land where all decisions will be in his favor. In the big diamond Johnny is "safe" at last.

Brought down by a cannon-speed ball hurled by Rogers, the Gull third sacker passed away in Mobile at 7:30 o'clock last night after being unconscious since Sunday. When first struck by the terrific drive fired by Tom Rogers, reports indicated that he would be able to recover.

Many other ball players have been hit, and many have recovered. But the Great Umpire had marked Johnny Dodge for an "out."

Though his critics had assailed him, there can be nothing now but uniform regret over his untimely end, just when he appeared to have recovered his grip upon himself. Endowed by nature with every attribute for success on the diamond, Johnny Dodge had apparently only coupled his latent faculties with self-mastery. When that juncture was reached his success was assured.

But this spring, when discarded by the Vols, Johnny Dodge blotted out the past and inserted a clean leaf upon which he was rapidly writing good deeds. Humbly, he confessed to a squandering of past opportunities and a determination to make his critics accord him the just praise of his new career.

Dodge had been criticized throughout his career as being indifferent towards baseball and labeled a happy-go-lucky person. He was described as one of the best fielders in the league "when he wanted to be." Dodge's personality attracted friends wherever he played, but his attitude and perseverance was always in question. Rogers regretted the incident, but was never blamed.

The newspaper explained the incident:

The position, which Johnny Dodge assumed at the plate and his habit of running out into the diamond to meet a curve before it broke, actually magnified his danger of being struck. He was not a batter who "culled" from the ball, but instead walked into it. It is highly probable that against Tom Rogers, Johnny set for a curve was "crossed" by a fast

SOME RULES

The following rules and regulations were adopted unanimously at the powder plant yesterday governing players in the Old Hickory baseball league:

"No crap games will be allowed while the games are in action; no bracelet watches shall be worn by any of the players, and all players shall be required to take at least one bath at the beginning of the season and one at the close."

These "rules" for the Old Hickory Baseball League actually appeared in the March 29, 1919 issue of the Tennessean. *Courtesy of the author.*

ball which he met with the full speed of the pitch. For Tom Rogers throws a terrifically fast ball. Yet rarely has he struck any batter.

The Vols won the Southern Association championship in 1916 while Rogers tied for the league lead with 24 wins (12 losses). Rogers made his major league debut the following season with the St. Louis Browns, appearing in 24 games (eight starts) with a 3-6 record a 3.89 ERA.

Rogers was sent to the Philadelphia A's during the 1918 season while ending his major league career in 1921 with the Yankees. His major league career record of 15-30 with a 3.95 ERA occurred in 83 games. Rogers also appeared in one game of the 1921 World Series while with the Yankees. Rogers died in Nashville on March 7, 1936.

Tom Wilson and the Nashville Elite Giants

Long forgotten is a Nashville baseball stadium that was demolished decades ago. Only the old-timers of the Nashville sporting community remember cozy Wilson Park. Wilson Park was built and owned by Tom Wilson, a black baseball team owner. Wilson was a Nashvillian and the pioneer for securing baseball for the black population of Nashville.

Wilson broke ground on the ballpark site in 1928, with construction completed in the spring of 1929. The ballpark was located in the Trimble Bottom section of Nashville, north of the fairgrounds, near the confluence of Second and Fourth Avenues. The ballpark, which accommodated 4,000 fans, was built in the largest section of Nashville's black community.

Wilson was born in Atlanta in 1890 and moved to Nashville with his parents as a youth. His parents studied medicine at Nashville's Meharry, the leading black medical school in the South at that time. Coming from an affluent family, Wilson reputedly became wealthy with his many entrepreneurial ventures.

It is said that his finances established himself as one of the wealthier citizens in Nashville—black or white. Not blessed with the greatest of ability as a player, Wilson became interested in baseball as a teen participating in the Nashville Capital League. The league was an industrial league, which stimulated semi-professional teams. During this period in 1914, Wilson became interested in the promotional side of the game. Totally on his own, he sponsored exhibition games between semi-professional teams.

In the spring of 1913, baseball Hall of Famer Rube Foster and his Chicago American Giants arrived in Nashville for an exhibition with a collection of NCL all-stars. The games played at Sulphur Dell drew the largest attendance

Nashville businessmen Tom Wilson was a major contributor to Nashville's early black baseball heritage. *Courtesy of the author.*

at that time for a black sporting event. The fan turnout encouraged Wilson to pursue his own team that he accomplished four years later.

Wilson started a semi-professional team, the Nashville Standard Giants that booked exhibitions in Tennessee and other Southern states. He acquired better players against tougher competition, enabling his reputation as a baseball man to prosper. In 1921, he enhanced his team's appearance by displaying new uniforms with jerseys that read across the front "Nashville Elite Giants."

The Elite Giants joined the Southern Negro League as a full-time enterprise. The league consisted of teams from Birmingham, New Orleans, Montgomery, Atlanta, Jacksonville and Chattanooga. The popularity of black baseball in the South was beginning to explode.

With the construction of Wilson Park, Wilson became the first black to own a stadium in the South and one of the first in the country. James Hendrix, a resident in the Wilson Park neighborhood, once wrote a passage in his pamphlet, *I Remember Tom.* The passage appeared in a 1999 article of *Black Ball News.*

"Whenever there would be a game, the word of mouth promotion would guarantee a good attendance. The nearby residents may as well be in attendance because the loud speakers would broadcast all the details and enthusiasm of the crowd for miles around. The activities at Wilson Park soon became so wide spread that the white spectators out numbered the black spectators."

Credit is given to Wilson's personality and some of his business interests with the white-owned businesses for helping to draw whites to Wilson Park.

One of these common interests was the Franklin Inter-Urban Transportation System that transported commuters between Nashville and Franklin.

Wilson Park was open to all community groups, black and white. Wilson's financial success and promotional work for his baseball team enabled him to reach a long-time goal. The Elite Giants were asked to join the Negro National League in 1930. The Great Depression had just begun with the 1929 Stock Market crash hampering Wilson's newest enterprise.

The members of the league struggled to survive, but managed to finish the 1930 season. With the economic future in doubt, the league attempted another season. Wilson surprised his patrons when he moved his team to Cleveland hoping to find more success in a larger city. The Elite Giants became the Cleveland Cubs in the National Negro League.

The league and the Cubs became insolvent during the 1931 season and the league folded. Wilson returned to Nashville, determined to conquer the depression. Wilson, along with several other team owners, reformed the Negro Southern League in 1932. He used Wilson Park to sponsor exhibition games with barnstorming attractions as the Ethiopian Clowns and Syd Pollock's Bearded Cuban House of David.

The 1935 Nashville Elite Giants was once members of the Negro National League that later moved to Baltimore. *Courtesy of the National Baseball Hall of Fame and Library, Cooperstown, New York.*

In 1933, Wilson joined an effort to re-establish the Negro National League. His team reverted back to the Nashville Elite Giants. It was also at this time that Wilson co-sponsored the leagues first East-West All Star Game to showcase the league. Eventually, Wilson moved the Elite Giants to Columbus and then Washington in 1936. They became the Baltimore Elite Giants in 1937 where they remained until after Jackie Robinson integrated baseball in 1947. The team's operations were always run from Nashville even when they were located in another city.

The league owners elected Wilson as their President of the Negro National League, a position he held for nearly 10 years. The league and the Elite Giants grew financially under his leadership. The best player he produced in Baltimore was future Dodger and Hall of Famer Roy Campanella.

Wilson's health began to deteriorate and he stepped down as league president in 1946. In spite of his poor health, he was persuaded to lead the Negro Southern League. With reservations, Wilson prepared to oversee the league's operation primarily from Nashville. On May 17, 1947 Wilson suffered a heart attack and died at his Nashville home.

Before his death, Wilson converted Wilson Park into a dog racing track and later the Paradise Ballroom, which attracted such celebrities as Duke Ellington and Louis Armstrong.

Wilson's personality and high spirits earned him the name "Smiling Tom" by his friends and fans that knew him. Satchel Paige, whose contract was purchased from the Birmingham Black Barons, played for Wilson in Cleveland. Many other future Hall of Famers' visits and exploits in Wilson Park have been lost to time and poor record keeping.

Wilson is buried in Nashville's Greenwood Cemetery. An historical marker was placed near the site of Wilson Park to honor Tom Wilson and his baseball presence in the city.

Nashville's Black Baseball Heritage

When Jackie Robinson broke the baseball color barrier playing for the Brooklyn Dodgers in 1947, black ball players finally had the chance to display their talents competing with the whites. For decades, many black players were good enough to make a major league roster, but were denied the chance. The black players were forced to organize their own teams and leagues.

Blacks were just as interested in the game of baseball as white people, as reported in the Nashville newspaper *Union and Dispatch* on December 21, 1866: "The colored young men of the city took base ball fever some time ago, and organized a club from the choicest material on hand, calling it the Excelsior. Having a high estimate of their skill in the national game, the Excelsiors have challenged every other club in the city, but unfortunately without any response."

By the early 1900s, the Capital League was the prominent league for Nashville blacks. Greenwood Park and Athletic Park played host to the Standard Giants – a semi-pro team. The black women organized a Nashville team named the Bloomer

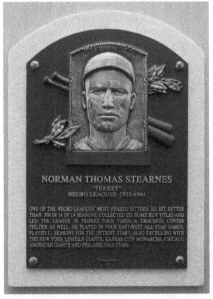

Norman "Turkey" Stearnes is the only Nashville-born baseball player enshrined in the National Baseball Hall of Fame, playing his entire career in the Negro Leagues. *Courtesy of the National Baseball Hall of Fame and Library, Cooperstown, New York.*

Girls that played for decades. Other established teams were the Black Sox, Eclipse, Athletics, Nationals and Baptist Hill Swifts.

There have been countless numbers of black players from Nashville who might have made it to the major leagues if given a chance. These are a few of them:

Norman "Turkey" Stearnes is the only baseball player born in Nashville that is a member of the National Baseball Hall of Fame. The powerful left-handed batter went to Pearl High School and played for several teams in the Negro Leagues including the Elite Giants (1920). After three seasons in the Negro Southern League, Stearnes joined the Detroit Stars (1923-31, 1933, 1937) slugging 35 home runs in 1923 and 50 the next year.

In his first nine seasons with Detroit, Stearnes' lowest batting average was .326; his high was .378. Stearnes led the Chicago American Giants to the first National Negro League championship as a leadoff batter, averaging .387. His play earned the top vote recipient among outfielders for the Black East-West All-Star game held in Comiskey Park. During his career, Stearnes collected seven home run titles and a .359 league average. Stearnes was credited with a .351 average in exhibition games against white teams.

Clinton "Butch" McCord was a first baseman/outfielder and played ball at Tennessee State before joining the Nashville Black Vols of the Negro Southern League in 1947. He joined the Baltimore Elite Giants in 1949 then joined "Double Day" Radcliffe's Chicago American Giants. As a Giant, McCord batted .359 in 1950. During his 11 seasons, McCord won two batting titles, two silver gloves, three pennants and three playoffs.

McCord displayed his great offensive skills with Paris of the Mississippi-Ohio Valley league while averaging .363 and .392. In these two seasons for Paris, he hit for power (16 and 15 home runs), showed speed (22 and 20 stolen bases), while driving in 118 and 109 runs. McCord would play in several minor leagues including the International League, American Association, Texas League, and South Atlantic League.

Bruce Petway was a catcher known for his strong accurate throwing arm. Petway played for the Cuban X-Giants (1906), Leland Giants (1906-10),

Chicago American Giants (1911-18) and Detroit Stars (1919-25). Petway gained notoriety when in 1910 he was playing an exhibition game in Cuba against the Detroit Tigers. Petway threw out Ty Cobb three times in three attempts trying to steal a base. He batted .390 in exhibition games against the Tigers.

Petway was considered the premier catcher in his day and the first outstanding receiver in black baseball history. He left his studies at Nashville's Meharry Medical College for a professional baseball career. Petway was part of a 1910 team (Chicago American Giants) put together by the immortal Rube Foster who thought it was the

Clinton "Butch" McCord played for the Nashville Cubs, Nashville Black Vols, Baltimore Elite Giants, Chicago American Giants and the minor leagues. *Courtesy of the late Butch McCord.*

greatest team ever assembled—black or white. Petway batted .397 that season. Foster brought his American Giants with Petway to Sulphur Dell for an exhibition in September 1913.

Henry Kimbro played for the Washington Elite Giants (1937), Baltimore Elite Giants (1938-40, 1942-51), New York Black Yankees (1941) and the Birmingham Black Barons (1952-53). Kimbro was blessed with speed and power that had a strong accurate arm in the outfield. In 1944, Kimbro batted .329 to led the league in stolen bases and one home run shy of tying leaders Josh Gibson and Buck Leonard.

Kimbro was a member of six all-star teams and averaged well over .300 for his career. By the time the color barrier was broken, Kimbro was 33 years old and considered too old for the majors. In the off-seasons, he was a star player in the Cuban League. After the National Negro League folded in 1948, Kimbro hit .352 and .370 in 1949-50 in the American Negro League.

Jim Zapp played for the Baltimore Elite Giants (1945-46, 1950-51, 1954), Nashville Cubs (1946), Atlanta Black Crackers (1947) and Birmingham Black Barons (1948, 1954). Zapp began playing baseball in 1942 in the Navy while stationed in Hawaii, and his Navy team won consecutive service ball championships (1943-44). Later, his 11 home runs with Atlanta in the Negro Southern League earned him a spot on the roster Barons, members of the Negro American League.

The outfielder had speed and played excellent defense, while making it to the minor leagues in 1952 with Paris in the Mississippi-Ohio Valley League. Zapp hit .330 and recorded 20 home runs with 136 RBIs (a league record). Two years later, he was with the Big Spring Broncs clubbing 32 home runs. Zapp played part of that season in Birmingham when the Negro Leagues were dying.

In 1955, he remained with Big Spring, batting .311 with 29 home runs and 90 RBIs. Zapp finished his professional career with the Port Arthur Sea Hawks collecting eight home runs and 37 RBIs. Making Nashville his home, Zapp played two seasons of semi-pro baseball (1948-49) in the city with the Morocco Stars and Nashville Stars.

Wesley "Doc" Dennis played for the Baltimore Elite Giants (1942-45, 1951), Philadelphia Stars (1949), Birmingham Black Barons (1950, 1952-55), and was considered an average player with great defensive skills with versatility. In 1949, Dennis moved back to Nashville and played for the Nashville Stars in a lesser league.

Dennis played in the infield, primarily at first base. His best seasons were with the Philadelphia Stars as the starting first baseman for three seasons. Dennis batted .288 and .247 in 1946-47. After his retirement from baseball, Dennis was known in Nashville as an outstanding golfer.

Even the breaking of the color barrier by Robinson could only limit the number of blacks on a major league roster. There was still prejudice and only eight teams in each league.

"Junior" Jim Gilliam began his baseball career with the Nashville Black Vols (1945) and Baltimore Elite Giants (1946-51) before entering the minor leagues and eventually the majors. Gilliam had a successful major league career with the Brooklyn and Los Angeles Dodgers (1953-66).

Gilliam had a lifetime batting average of .265 with 65 home runs and 558 RBIs and named the NL Rookie of the Year (1953). The speedster was the Dodgers' leadoff hitter for most of the 1950s and scored over 100 runs in his first four seasons. Once Gilliam led the league in triples and walks.

Gilliam was a two-time All-Star (1956, 1957), and a member of four World Series champion teams (1955, 1959, 1963 and 1965). He died in 1978, after serving as a long-time coach. The Dodgers then retired his number.

On July 28, 2015, the Sounds' First Tennessee Park address that was 401 Jackson Street officially became 19 Junior Gilliam Way.

In this writer's opinion, Gilliam is the best baseball player—black or white—born in Nashville.

"Junior" Jim Gilliam was the National League Rookie of the Year (1953) and a two-time All-Star. *Courtesy of the author.*

Nashville Welcomes the Great Babe Ruth

After the Baltimore-born George Herman Ruth arrived in major league baseball the game was never the same. The beloved Babe Ruth would become a legend with his powerful bat and off-the-field personality.

Nashville fans were entertained in the 1920's and 1930's with "The Sultan of Swat" and his exploits. Before First Tennessee Park was built on a portion of the former site where the old Sulphur Dell ballpark once stood, there was an historical marker indicating Nashville's contribution to America's pastime.

The State Capital Building from the South prominently overlooks this site, which for a long time was a parking lot. Perhaps there should be an historical marker on this once sacred plot that reads: "Babe Ruth Parked A Few Here." Ruth did park a few over the outfield fence.

A yearly routine of major league teams heading North from their Southern spring training camps was to stop and play exhibition games in cities along the way.

Nashville was a frequent stop for the New York Yankees, who played at Sulphur Dell several times in the 1920's and 30's. The Bronx Bombers sometimes played the hometown Vols in those games or other major league teams. One of the most memorable visits by the Yankees to Nashville was in April 1931, where Ruth blasted his last home run at the Dell against the Nashville Vols.

Ruth began the first day of that visit in Nashville swinging a golf club instead of a bat. He was invited to play a round of golf at the Belle Meade Country Club. A foursome of Ruth and three prominent Nashvillians played the 18-hole course with a small gallery of invited guests. Ruth, wearing gray knickers and a white sweatshirt on this chilly Easter Sunday morning, carded an 81.

In 1931, Yankees manager Joe McCarthy was in his inaugural season with the team. Teammates accompanying Ruth included future Hall of Famers Lou Gehrig, Tony Lazzeri, and Bill Dickey.

Approximately 4,000 Nashvillians witnessed Yankees' pitcher Roy Sherid face pitcher George Milstead and his Vols in the afternoon exhibition—the first of a two-game series. Nashville jumped out to a 4-3 lead after two innings. Ruth, who was 37 years old and in the final year of an $80,000 contract, slammed the first pitch from Milstead over the right centerfield fence in the third inning for a home run. The dinger by Ruth was only his second of the spring in more than twenty games.

The beloved Babe Ruth made several visits to Nashville when his New York Yankees played exhibition games in the city. *Courtesy of the New York Yankees.*

The fans exploded to their feet with excitement as Ruth rounded the bases in his trademark home run trot. Ruth left the game at the end of seven innings where he played the infamous right field "dump." He finished the game 2-for-3 with a single, walk, home run, and a strikeout as the Yanks erupted for eight runs in their half of the ninth to win, 14-8. First baseman Gehrig was hitless in six trips to the plate. The Vols contributed to the loss by committing seven errors mostly by rookies.

The next day, the Yankees demolished the Vols 23-3 with a 25 hit barrage to conclude this two-game series. Gehrig was 3-for-5 and scored five runs. The Babe failed to homer in five plate appearances, but collected two hits during the game. He bashed one of his singles off the right field wall with such velocity that one of the wooden planks was knocked loose.

The Babe's visits to Sulphur Dell included plenty of thrills. These are Ruth's appearances in Nashville as a player:

April 1924: An overflowing crowd of 12,000 Nashvillians witnessed the exhibition between the Brooklyn Dodgers and the Yankees. The then-record crowd watched Ruth receive as a gift a large twist of Tennessee tobacco. Ruth also tossed signed baseballs into the stands. His only hit in the game was a shot off the pitcher's leg for a single. Ruth also walked twice in a 1-for-3 day. Final score: Yankees 8, Dodgers 8.

April 1925: This was a two-game series, once again involving the Yankees and Brooklyn. Ruth visited 700 orphans at the Dell after the first day. He recorded a triple off the center field wall in a 2-for-3 afternoon. Final score: Yankees 10, Dodgers 7.

The next day, Ruth's only hit was a single up the middle in a Brooklyn 9-8 victory. The fans roared as Ruth showed his arm by throwing out a runner at the plate from right field. Gehrig, who had brief stints in the majors the previous two years, was 0-for-1 as a pinch-hitter in what would be his first full season.

April 1926: Ruth was hitless in another duel with the Brooklyn Dodgers an 11-4 Yankees win. Gehrig blasted a centerfielder home run, which was said the longest ever hit at Sulphur Dell.

April 1927: This Yankee team became perhaps the greatest baseball team of all time. Ruth hit a home run, pleasing the fans in a 10-8 loss to the St. Louis Cardinals. The ball sailed over the right field fence in a 1-for-3 afternoon. Ruth would total 60 home runs that season, a record that would stand until 1961. Manager Miller Huggins' club would end the season with an amazing 110-44 record. They capped off the year with a four-game sweep over the Pirates in the World Series.

April 1928: Facing the hometown Vols, Ruth batted clean up and drilled a two-run shot over the right field fence. Second baseman Leo Durocher, another future Hall of Famer, was 2-for-4 in his second of three years with the Yankees. The Vols won the 10-inning game, 11-10.

April 1930: Yankee pitcher Waite Hoyt, a former Vols player, beat Nashville 8-3 as catcher Bill Dickey slugged two home runs. Ruth was 0-for-2 with three walks as the crowd jeered at each pass. However, during batting practice Ruth put on a display with baseballs flying over and off the fences. The farthest blast was reported to have landed in the horse lot in the back of the icehouse.

April 1933: Yankee hurler Red Ruffing shut out the Vols in a 13-0 rout. Ruth collected two singles as he was in the twilight of his career. Ruth played before a crowd of 3,500 in a season, which was to pay him $52,000.

April 1934: The Babe made his last appearances as a player when the Yankees faced the Vols in a two-game series. Ruth, in his final year with the Yankees, hit the right field screen for a double and added a single. Final score: Vols 5, Yankees 4.

In what would be the last game for Ruth in Nashville, he singled twice in three at-bats. The Vols won the second game, 6-5. A reporter walked in on Ruth in his hotel room before the game and overheard

Babe Ruth with Belle Meade Country Club's golf pro George Livingstone during the Bambino's 1931 visit to Nashville. *Courtesy of the Belle Meade Country Club.*

"The Bambino" complaining about having to get up so early in the morning (10:30 a.m.). The reporter noticed Ruth's breakfast of scrambled eggs, ham, toast and sausage on two plates. Later he smoked a morning cigar.

Blinky Horn, sportswriter for The *Nashville Tennessean*, expressed the feelings of all baseball fans that came in contact with the great legend. After watching Ruth at Sulphur Dell, Horn wrote:

Hobbling around on his damaged hoof, Babe Ruth could not have suffered the anguish, which penetrated the bosoms of the Kid Klan yesterday when the Great Bam failed to punch one out of reach. Next to carrying water for the elephants there is no thrill, which sets the pulse of the urchins fluttering like to viewing Babe Ruth larruping a home run. Proudly clutching a baseball upon which Babe Ruth had scrawled his name a pair of youngsters yesterday came past the seat in which we sat.

There gleamed in their eye a light that only comes only to those who have mingled with a monarch. Being a king is a bore some business. But being a king worshipper is something which makes the heart skip sidewise. Babe Ruth has done many a thing, which has brought him no testimonials from moral up lifters. But he is the idol of kid land and always will be regardless of what he may do to displease the reformers.

Ruth would finish the 1934 season with the Yankees, then exhaust an ill-fated 1935 season with the lowly Boston Braves before retiring. The Babe, who began his career as a pitcher with the Red Sox in 1914, finished his 22-year career with 714 home runs and a .342 lifetime batting average. Ruth was inducted into the National Baseball Hall of Fame in Cooperstown in 1936 as part of the inaugural group.

Nashville's Walter Heckman was 13 years old when he met Ruth during one of the 1934 games at Sulphur Dell. He possessed a baseball that was signed by several St. Louis Cardinals he collected a year earlier. The late Heckman pursued Ruth for his precious signature on that ball that he possessed until his death at age 88 in 2009.

"My brother, a friend and I rode the streetcar downtown and walked to Sulphur Dell," said Heckman. "We thought since Babe Ruth was coming to town, it would be nice to have his signature. Our second choice was Bill Dickey, and of course we wanted Lou Gehrig's autograph. We couldn't get Gehrig's because he was in the outfield shagging flys.

"Babe had just finished his workout and was sitting in the dugout all sweaty just like a big man would be. As we walked down to the first base dugout steps we asked the man on the gate if we could get Babe Ruth's signature on a ball. He let us down there. There was Babe sitting with several other players. We asked him if he'd sign our ball. He said, 'Sure, kid.' And he was smiling and as sweaty as could be. We thanked him and he said 'sure, anytime.'

"As long as I'm alive, that ball will not be sold. After I'm gone my heirs can do whatever they want with it. It was like being in the presence of Jesus Christ. I know that might sound sacrilegious, but for three kids in our generation being in the presence of Babe Ruth was almost like being in the presence of Jesus Christ."

Ruth died of throat cancer on Aug. 16, 1948, leaving behind a legacy like no baseball player before or since. Fortunately, for Nashville baseball fans "The Babe" left a little of that legacy right here in Nashville, Tennessee.

Sulphur Dell's First Night Game

The first night baseball game (with permanent lights) in Nashville was played on May 18, 1931 at the Sulphur Dell ballpark. In the previous year, the Southern Association's first night game was played in Little Rock, Ark. Speculation was that night games would attract more fans through the turnstiles, but baseball purist supporting day baseball claimed bugs would be the main attraction.

The Nashville Vols played the Mobile Marines in this historic Monday night occasion. Nashville sports writing legend Fred Russell gave this preview in the *Nashville Banner*.

The greatest throng to ever witness a game in Sulphur Dell is expected Monday night when the Volunteers of Joe Klugman oppose the Mobile Marines in the first game of Southern League night baseball offered in Nashville and the state of Tennessee. Reduced railroad and bus rates are bringing in hundreds of bugs from neighboring towns, and it is thought that close to 10,000 will be on hand to see the curtain rise on baseball a la nocturnal.

The final test of the lighting system in the Dell was made Sunday night and everything pronounced in readiness for the Monday night opener. The gates will open at 6 p.m. A band will offer selections between seven and eight o'clock when the boys are taking batting and fielding practice. The game is scheduled to start at 8 o'clock, but there are a few preliminaries on the program before actual play begins.

The Vols' starting pitcher was Frank Pearce, facing Mobile's veteran Rube "Red" Oldham, who was also the acting manager. Oldham was in the twilight of his career, playing in the major leagues from 1914 through 1926 with Detroit and Pittsburgh.

This photo is from the first night game in Sulphur Dell. The reflections of the lights are prominent as outdoor sports night photography was poor at this time. *Courtesy of the Metropolitan Government Archives of Nashville and Davidson County.*

Oldham scattered five hits in his complete-game 8-1 win over the Vols. The second batter of the game, Mobile leftfielder John Hutson, set the trend by belting a home run over the right centerfield wall. The ball sailed over the Hill Electric Company sign, which was a salute to the installers of the new lighting system.

More problems occurred mostly for the Vols and a portion of the estimated 7,000 fans, according to newspaper reports.

Although the Vols bats were not busy, bats were busy flying around trying to discover what it was all about. They were very annoying to the gents in the press box. These bats were far more annoying than Vols bats to Red Oldham.

The Vols committed six errors and managed their only run in the home half of the ninth inning. There was a theory that young pitchers perform better at night than under the sun, but that was shot down when the veteran Oldham beat the Vols' youngster Pearce. It was reported that this night game attracted more wives with their husbands than ever before. The reasons suggested that maybe the women came "to checkup on hubby and see if he was really going to a ball game."

Blinkey Horn of the *Tennessean* gave this report:

A heap of folks were present because the novelty of night baseball lured them into Sulphur Dell. No telling how many people who never saw a ball game before and never will again were there. After the sample of last night their curiosity is cured. After the comical exhibition Those Vols gave their desire to watch the hemophiliacs in action has had a set-back. It's hard enough for Those Vols to play winning ball by daylight. When the lights are turned on they merely grope around. Last night they blew out a fuse and were short-circuited.

A heap of people declared that they were sorry that they did not stay home and listen to Amos and Andy. Still it is doubtful if Amos and Andy could be any funnier than Those Vols were last night. They went through the blindfold test.

Other than the bats and bugs lacking in day games, night games featured problems. Kids were told that any baseball hit outside the ballpark would gain them free admission upon retrieval. After scrambling for the baseball one of these youths gave his opinions of the flying ball coming out of the night sky.

"It won't do at all," complained one of the boys. "You can't see the ball 'til it's right on you. It comes down busting out of the dark. It ain't worth the risk!"

When Vols' third baseman Johnny Chapman missed a pop fly by six feet after circling around the infield grass, a fan with a "fog horn voice" could be heard hollering:

"I knew it," he screamed. "They can't see those high ones." After another fly hit into the outfield this brave spectator shouted, "Watch him muff it." The centerfielder did muff it.

The newspapers reported more of the festivities surrounding the game.

A boy perched far out on the limb off a Fourth Avenue tree had to hear his country's song through in a combination sitting-prone posture. To have uncovered his head would have been fatal. He had to hold that limb.

Why, there was even a cheer leader in the audience. Along about the fifth inning a deadly serious gentleman left his seat and pranced boyishly up and down before the grandstand, exhorting the people to "Come on and give 'em some sand. They can't win the game unless we give them some sand."

Astonishingly, he was cold sober. Unkind remarks eventually retired him to his seat, a disillusioned, life-soured man. "They don't need sand, they need runs," was one of the cruel remarks. A terse "razzpberry" was the other.

Two very attractive young heartthrobs demanded that the folks stand up and stretch in the Vols' half of the lucky seventh. They stood alone for awhile, but persistence, aided and abetted by pulchritude, ultimately got them a supporting cast.

Habit claimed at least two victims, "Smokey Joe" Sewell, for the Vols and Kelly for the Marines, enjoyed brief naps. Sewell snored off first and was erased. Kelly snored off the same station and his energy-restoring snooze enabled the homelings to score their only run.

The next night would draw a disappointing attendance of 1,000 fans. However the Vols' bats finally came to life. Vols' pitcher George Milstead was spotted a 13 -2 lead after five innings when the Mobile club went to work on Milstead. They cut the lead to 13-11 entering the ninth.

With two men on base, Milstead, who was nearly yanked in the seventh, held on for the Vols first night victory. The only reported complaint was by the players objecting to a streetlight. A street lamp on Fourth Avenue

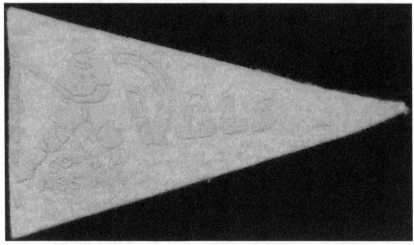

This is a Nashville Vols pennant circa. 1930s. *Courtesy of Jeremy Jones.*

was in the line of the batter behind the pitching mound blurring their sight. Nashville Mayor Hilary E. Howse, who was at the game, ordered the light to be extinguished.

Russell was a 25-year-old sports writer who was about to complete his second year at the *Banner.* His column "Sideline Sidelights," reflected his thoughts on the Nashville Vols new venture into night baseball.

Now that the Vols have gone into competition with the movies by staging their performances during the after dinner hours, it follows that they should keep space of their indoor rivals in the matter of ballyhoo. Today this department is offering a few suggestions that may be of help to the Vol management in the matter of increasing the box-office receipts.

The first thing Bob Allen and Company should do is to institute the "trailer" system. You know, like the talkies do in telling of next week's attraction. For instance, after the game tonight the baseballers should give a little sample of what may or will happen Tuesday night. The man with the megaphone would announce the following:

You saw Charlie Willis when he let down the champion Chicks with four hits. You've seen him breeze through the Barons. But get a look at him Tuesday night in that show of shows 'Telling It to the Marines.' See Willis in this ideal role.

It starts with a bang and rollicks pepfully along through reels of gayety to a splendid climax. There's pathos and drama, too. This well-constructed vehicle gives the star every opportunity to run that well-known gamut of emotions. And how Charlie runs them is nobody's business except the extra cashiers that will be necessary to count the box office receipts. DON'T MISS IT.

The minor and Negro Leagues were the first to play baseball in the evening. The majors followed in 1935, with their first night game in Cincinnati. Reportedly, Nashville's Wilson Park hosted black ball games at night close to the 1931 date. Due to the limited press coverage of black baseball, proper documentation on its first night game cannot be substantiated.

The Gilbert Family Contributes to Nashville Baseball

In 1901, the Southern Association was organized with the Vols as a charter member. The Vols won four pennants from that inaugural year through 1916. After that Nashville did not win another pennant until 1940.

After the 1938 season, Larry Gilbert was persuaded to leave his successful Southern Association team in New Orleans and come to Nashville. Gilbert had been the Pelicans' manager since 1923 and had become a Southern Association legend.

Vols team owner Fay Murray offered Gilbert part ownership in the Nashville franchise and become field manager beginning in 1939. A new era of history was about to be written in Nashville baseball.

Gilbert's first exposure to professional baseball was as a scoreboard boy at old Athletic Park in his hometown of New Orleans. At age 18, he signed his first professional contract with Victoria of the Texas League. Later, the Boston Braves drafted him as an outfielder.

In 1914, he played 72 games with the Braves and was a member of their roster against the Philadelphia Athletics in the 1914 World Series. Gilbert walked in his only World Series plate appearance as the Braves swept the A's in four games.

Subsequently, the New Orleans Pelicans of the Southern Association purchased his contract. After the 1919 season, he rejected an opportunity to sign with Cleveland in order to stay in New Orleans.

Gilbert became the Pelicans' manager in 1923 where he won the Southern Association championship in his first season. New Orleans won four Southern

Charlie Gilbert (left) with his father Larry the Vols manager who won four championships in Nashville. *Courtesy of Derby S. Gisclair and Helen Gilbert.*

Association championships under his guidance through the 1938 season (in 1932, he was their business manager).

Gilbert is credited with bringing the Vols into the golden age of baseball with his arrival in Nashville. The Vols ended a 23-year championship drought in Gilbert's second season. In his 10 seasons as the Vols' manager Gilbert recorded four league championships and numerous playoff victories.

The Southern Association adopted a playoff system in 1935 in which the first four teams competed to determine the league's representative against the winner of the Texas League. This was referred as the Shaughnessy Playoff. The Dixie Series involved the representatives from the Texas League and Southern Association.

During his tenure, Gilbert guided the Vols to four Southern championships, four Shaughnessy titles, and three Dixie championships. Gilbert finished his managerial career in 1948 with a championship.

In 1949, Gilbert moved into the Vols' front office as general manager. He sold his financial interest in the team to Ted Murray, the son of Fay Murray, in 1955. Gilbert then retired to his hometown of New Orleans after 45 years in professional baseball.

As one might expect, there were plenty of players who played under Gilbert who went on to the major leagues. Former major leaguer Johnny Sain was a benefactor of Gilbert's connections. Sain was a member of the Nashville Vols in 1940-41 while they were independents.

"Larry Gilbert was one of the finest men I ever knew," Sain said. "I was a free agent after being in the Tigers' organization. A friend of mine who was in Little Rock, made arrangements for me to go to spring training with Larry Gilbert.

"I played in the outfield when I didn't pitch, since I could hit line-drives fairly well. Gilbert was a super person, as far as I am concerned. Because of him I had the opportunity to play with the Braves. I was just fortunate to have had contact with him."

Sain's major league career spanned 11 seasons with the Boston Braves and Yankees. He recorded 139 wins and four World Series appearances. Gilbert's character and positive influence on Sain remained with him until his former manager's death.

On February 19, 1965, just two days after Gilbert's death, the *Boston Globe* carried the following story and headline: "Gilbert Debt Paid With Sain." The article read:

In the late 1920's, Larry Gilbert who ran the New Orleans Pelicans sold Bob Quinn of the Red Sox a southpaw pitcher who was a bust. This incident had a lot to do with the Boston Braves winning the pennant in 1948. Because he felt obligated, Gilbert in 1942, sent Quinn, then head of the impoverished Braves (Quinn was now Braves team owner), a tall angular young hurler (Sain) whose manner showed that he meant business.

"Johnny Sain was on trial, but after he had allowed only two runs in fifteen innings in spring training pitching, the Braves bought him at a fair price just before the season started. Sain won 20 games in 1946, 21 in 1947, 24 in 1948, then beat Bob Feller 1-0 in the first game of the World Series. Gilbert had paid his debt with interest but that is the sort of fellow he was, a capable, popular minor league executive in office, but a big leaguer at heart.

Harold "Tookie" Gilbert also played for his father in the 1949 season leading the Southern Association in hits (197). *Courtesy of Derby S. Gisclair and Helen Gilbert.*

Larry Gilbert was not the only Gilbert to wear a Nashville Vols uniform. Charlie and Harold "Tookie" Gilbert, his sons, played for him as Vols. Both had standout seasons in Nashville. His oldest son, Larry, Jr. died in Nashville in 1941.

Charlie had a major league career, which began in 1940 with Brooklyn and spanned six years, mostly as a utility player. He also played for the Cubs and Phillies. Charlie ended his career as a .229 lifetime hitter.

Charlie finished his playing career playing for his father and enjoyed a spectacular season in 1948 as a Vol. During the first four games, Charlie walloped seven home runs, setting a league record for most home runs in four consecutive games.

The 1948 Southern Association All-Star game featured the league leader against a collective group of players from the remaining teams in the league. Charlie smashed a 12th-inning solo home run to give the league leading Vols a 4-3 triumph over the All-Stars.

Charlie totaled 42 home runs for the Vols that season and helped his father win his fourth league championship. After the season, he was drafted by the Braves, but retired because of a back injury. He joined his father as a front office assistant for the Vols.

Tookie Gilbert was 10 years younger than his brother, and hit 33 home runs in 1949 for the Vols while leading the league in hits (197) and runs scored (146). On July 6, 1949, he became the 14th Vols player to hit three home runs in a game. Like his brother the year before, he helped lead the Vols to the league championship.

Tookie was property of the New York Giants and spent parts of the 1950 and 1953 seasons with the big league team. In 183 games his career average in the majors was .203. Tookie retired from baseball and became a sheriff in New Orleans.

Charlie Gilbert died in 1983 at age 64 and Tookie passed away in 1967 at age 38.

What did Larry Gilbert say was his formula for success?

"Make winning so pleasant and losing so unpleasant that hustle is automatic," Gilbert once said.

That theory worked well. The record books back him up.

The 1940 Nashville Vols: An All-Time Great Team

Baseball historians Bill Weiss and Marshall Wright once presented a list of the top 100 minor league teams of all-time. Listed at No. 47 were the 1940 Nashville Vols, a ballclub that posted a 101-47 record.

One of the keys to the 1940 Vols success was a great pitching staff, which included Cletus (Boots) Poffenberger, Leo Twardy, George Jeffcoat, Ace Adams, and Johnny Sain.

Poffenberger once thrilled Nashville baseball fans on Labor Day that year with a rare feat for a pitcher. He produced two wins in a doubleheader at Sulphur Dell to secure the Southern Association pennant for the hometown club.

In the first game, he earned the win with an inning of relief. In the nightcap, Poffenberger recorded a 10-2 victory. Those were Poffenberger's 24th and 25th victories of the season that helped send the 1940 Vols into the history books with one of the greatest minor league seasons ever.

This was only the third team in Southern Association history to be on top of the standings from wire-to-wire. The 101-47 record and a nine-and-a-half game-winning margin were maintained not only to pitching, but also a near flawless defense and a slugging lineup. Manager Larry Gilbert's leadership was the last key ingredient of this championship team.

The 1940 season began with a special train ride from Nashville to Atlanta, site of the Vols' opening day. The train consisted of 300 Nashvillians, including Mayor Thomas Cummings, city officials and fans. There was an omen of what was about to occur when the first three Vols' batters hit safely. Nashville won 12-8 against the Crackers and never looked back during the season.

Another league leader that season for the Vols was right-handed pitcher Ace Adams. Adams went 13-5 with a 4.06 ERA and led the league in strikeouts (122). Ace is not a nickname; it's his given name.

Adams pitched in Nashville for three years. His 13 victories were fourth best in the Vols rotation from that championship season. Adams appeared in 44 games (19 starts) tossed two shutouts with six complete games.

The following year, Adams was on the roster of the National League's New York Giants. In a six-year career, Adams was 41-33 with a 3.47 ERA in 302 games. Only seven of these games were as a starter. Adams led the league in saves (1944-45) and appearances (1942-43-44) while with the Giants.

Johnny Sain was used by Gilbert as a spot starter on the mound, a reliever and rightfielder. He appeared in 30 games (seven starts) posting an 8-4 record. Sain recorded a 4.45 ERA with one shutout and three complete games.

Gilbert arranged for Sain to gain a tryout with the Boston Braves of the National League in 1942. He appeared in 40 games, mostly in relief, earning a 4-7 record. Sain's baseball career was interrupted with three years in the

The 1940 Nashville Vols 101-47 record were the best in the team's history. *Courtesy of the Metropolitan Government Archives of Nashville and Davidson County.*

military. Sain became a Braves' starter in 1946, compiling a 20-14 record with a 2.21 ERA. In 1948, Sain had his best year in the majors with a 24-15 record leading the league in wins, complete games (28) and innings pitched (315).

Sain was also named the National League Pitcher-of-the-Year. His 11-year major league totals include a 136-116 record with a 3.45 ERA in 412 games. Sain also appeared in four World Series with the Braves and Yankees, going 2-2 in six starts.

Another key to the Vols success was its continuity. The starting lineup remained intact throughout the season, with only two roster changes to the pitching staff in mid-season. Several players were veterans with prior major league experience. Sain was the only player to reach major league stardom, while only one player failed to reach the major leagues.

The rest of the 1940 Nashville lineup:

First base—Mickey Rocco set the league record for the most double plays by a first baseman at 179. He recorded a .305 average, clubbed 21 home runs while driving in 101 runs. Rocco's 18-year baseball career includes four years with Cleveland (1943-46) where he batted .258. In 1944, he led the American League with 653 plate appearances.

Second base—John Mihalic was the Vols leadoff batter and led the league with 127 walks, which was a league record at that time. He batted .317, was second in the league with runs scored (133) and third in doubles (54). Mihalic also set a league record for double plays by a second baseman with 143. The 10-year Southern Association veteran also batted .244 with the Washington Senators (1935, 36, 37).

Shortstop—Dick Culler also set a league mark for double plays by a shortstop. He batted .277 with 73 runs-batted-in and only one home run. Later, he became the Boston Braves regular shortstop in 1945-46. Culler spent eight years in the major leagues with five different teams. His major league career totals a .244 average in 472 games.

Third base—Bob Boken was a 32-year-old veteran whose 118 runs-batted-in tied for the league lead. He also recorded a .302 batting average while collecting 13 home runs.

This veteran appeared with the Washington Senators (1933-34) and Chicago White Sox (1934). Boken was a .247 hitter in 457 career at-bats on the major league level.

Catcher—Charley "Greek" George set a Southern Association for a catcher with a .998 fielding percentage, making one error in 612 chances with two passed balls. The record stood until 1961 when the league folded. George batted .335 with nine home runs and 109 runs-batted-in. His difficulty with major league pitching limited his time there. Playing for five different teams (1935, 36, 38, 41, 45), he managed a .177 batting average in 118 games. While playing for the Philadelphia Athletics in 1945, he slugged an umpire in the nose during an argument. George was given a one-year suspension and never played another major league game.

Centerfield—Oris Hockett led the Vols in batting with a .363 average, 14 home runs and 68 runs-batted-in. He finished eight points behind the league leader for average, finishing third. Prior to joining the Vols, Hockett played two years with the Brooklyn Dodgers. After the 1940 season, he played five seasons with the Cleveland Indians. Hockett had a .276 lifetime batting average and represented the Indians in the 1944 All-Star game.

Rightfielder—Gus Dugas was the Vols' third outfielder and was 33 years old when he batted .336, hit 22 home runs and 118 runs-batted-in. His home run and RBI totals tied him for the league's best. Dugas' major league experience includes short stints with the Pittsburgh Pirates (1930, 32, 33) and Washington Senators (1934). He hit .206 in 125 games, but had a .327 career minor league batting average.

Pitcher—Boots Poffenberger was the ace of the staff, leading the league with a 26-9 record. He appeared in 38 games (33 starts) completing 18 games with three shutouts. Remarkably, his 4.58 ERA was the second worst of the pitching staff. Prior to joining the Vols in 1940, Poffenberger played three years in the majors with Detroit (1937-38) and Brooklyn (1939). His big league career totals include a 16-12 record with a 4.75 ERA in 57 games. After two years in Nashville he spent three years in the military, then retired in 1946 after playing in San Diego. Poffenberger was a favorite with his teammates. His favorite breakfast consisted of two fried eggs and a beer.

From the Desk of
John Sain

Dear Bill

Ever since I heard the statement that Lou Gehrig made where he said "I am the luckiest person on the face of the earth" I have always considered myself as being one of those people. I have often thought how nice it would be to sit down with Larry Gilbert, Casey Stengle and Bill Southworth and tell them how much they did for me and how much I appreciated what they did for me as a player.

Also Ralph Houk gave me a chance to be a pitching coach for which I enjoyed as much as a player, eleven years as a player and 16 years as a coach , 4 world series as player and 5 world series as a coach.

I realize yesterdays news is dead news. Thank you for being interested . You bring back a lot of pleasant memories. Hope you have a large waste basket for all of this stuff.

Sincerely

John Sain
August 27, 2001

Pitcher Johnny Sain was used by Larry Gilbert as a spot starter, posting an 8-4 record in 30 appearances. *Courtesy of the author.*

Pitcher—Leo Twardy was the only regular never to reach the major leagues. He was second on the team with 17 wins (11 losses). Twardy appeared in 53 games and recorded a 3.45 ERA.

Pitcher—George Jeffcoat recorded a 14-6 season with a 3.78 ERA. The right-hander was second only to teammate Adams in strikeouts with 121.

Jeffcoat opened the 1940 playoffs striking out 18 Chattanooga Lookouts in a Vols' 6-1 victory. At one time, he struck out seven Lookouts in a row for a league record. As a major leaguer, he was 7-11 in parts of four years with Brooklyn (1936, 37, 39) and the Boston Braves (1943). In his 70 career games he recorded a 4.51 ERA while pitching mostly in relief.

Those 1940 Nashville Vols went on to win the Shaughnessy Playoffs and the Dixie Series. The Shaughnessy consisted of a postseason playoff within the Southern Association to determine the representative to the Dixie Series. The Dixie Series was played between the champions of the Southern Association and the Texas League.

The Sporting News also named Gilbert their Minor League Manager-of-the-Year for 1940.

Nashville's All-Star Games

Nashville has been host to several professional baseball All-Star games, beginning in the 1940s, and involving the Nashville Vols. That league began playing an All-Star game in 1938. The league leader at a selected July date would host a collection of All-Star players from the rest of the league members.

The 1940 Nashville Vols were on their way to a Southern Association pennant when they hosted their first All-Star game at Sulphur Dell on July 8. Led by manager Larry Gilbert, the Vols lost that game, 6-1.

A hard rain in Nashville delayed the start of the game and kept the attendance down to 6,000 fans. Paul Richards was the player/manager of the Atlanta Crackers and belted a solo home run in the second inning to give the All-Stars a 2-0 lead. The clout by Richards was reported in *The Tennessean* "hit a street car in Jackson Street and rebounded into the park."

The All-Stars blasted 17 hits off of four Nashville pitchers for the easy win. Vols third baseman Bob Boken belted a second inning home run for the home team, preventing a shutout. Boken's home run was reported in the newspaper as the second longest home run ever hit at Sulphur Dell. The distance was reported as 420 feet over the left-centerfield wall. Boots Poffenberger, who would register a record 26 wins for the Vols that season, took the loss.

July 9, 1943, the country was at war. Baseball was not interrupted, but was greatly affected, as the major league rosters were diluted while players became soldiers. Nashville hosted its second Southern Association All-Star game at this time. In his fifth season at the Vols helm, Gilbert led the Vols to their first All-Star win, 3-2 in front of 9,350 Sulphur Dell fans.

This ticket is from the 1948 All-Star game played in Nashville where Vols' Charlie Gilbert slammed a walk-off home run for a victory. *Courtesy of the author.*

Glenn Gardner, a 12-game winner at the All-Star break, went the distance for the Vols. The Southern Stars scored a run in the first inning, but a throwing error in the fifth inning by losing Birmingham pitcher Howard Fox enabled Nashville to tie the score at 1-1. The Vols recorded back-to-back singles by Mizel Platt and Mel Hicks in the sixth frame placing runners at first and second with one out.

Fox followed by unleashing two wild pitches to score Platt and put Hicks on third base. Vols hitters Ed Sauer and Pete Elko walked to load the bases. After Fox was mercifully relieved on the mound, Johnny Mihalic singled to score Hicks that eventually proved to be the winning run. The Stars scored a ninth-inning run for the game's final tally.

The proceeds of the game amounted to $5,646, which was donated to a war relief fund. War bonds were given to each Nashville Vols player and each All-Star. Four members of the All-Star team and two umpires failed to appear at the game due to the late arrival of the famous "Dixie Flyer" train. The Vols continued their winning ways and won the 1943 Southern Association pennant.

Gilbert would enter the Vols' 1948 season as his 10th in Nashville and 25th overall in the Southern Association. In what would be his last season as a manager, Gilbert once again led his first-place club against the Southern All-Stars at Sulphur Dell on July 20. This mid-season Southern classic would be the most memorable for the league and Gilbert.

Charlie Gilbert, oldest son of the Vols manager, had been playing major league baseball since 1940. Charlie joined the Vols after 1947 and a season with the Philadelphia Phillies.

Vols rightfielder Charlie Workman slugged a two-run fifth inning home run to open the scoring. Nashville added a run in the seventh to take a 3-0 lead into the ninth. Ben Wade started the game for the Vols, shutting out the All-Stars through five innings and was relieved by Leo Twardy in the sixth.

Twardy gave up two singles and a walk to begin the ninth. Pete Mallory relieved Twardy and faced his first batter, future Boston Red Sox star Walt Dropo of the Stars. Dropo hit an apparent double-play ball to Vols' second baseman, Buster Boguskie. But the throw to second was off-line and the Stars scored their first run while the bases remained full.

Mickey Rutner followed with a double off the center field wall to tie the game 3-3, forcing extra innings. The game remained tied until the bottom of the 12th. Charlie Gilbert took his turn at bat and the *Tennessean* described the game-winner.

Little Charlie Gilbert hit one for the ol' man last night. The Vol centerfielder smashed a drive over the right field wall in the last of the 12th inning to give Those Vols a thrilled-packed 4-3 triumph over the All-Stars in the annual league classic before the paying patrons in Sulphur Dell.

"Young Gilbert's wall wallop, his 28th of the year, gave Larry Gilbert, Vol manager, probably the biggest thrill he has ever received from watching his son hit a home run.

Mallory was credited with the victory. Larry Gilbert resigned as the Vols manager at the end of the season and became vice president and general manager. Nashville also won the Southern Association pennant. Workman led the league with 52 home runs and 182 RBIs. Smokey Burgess led the league in batting with a .386 average for the Vols.

The Vols would host their next All-Star game at Sulphur Dell July 12, 1949. Rollie Hemsley was now the Nashville manager and had maneuvered his club into first place. More than 11,000 Nashville fans witnessed a game in which 10 All-Star records were broken.

The Vols were embarrassed 18-6, with the Stars scoring nine runs in the ninth to break open the game. Three Nashville pitchers (Frankie Marino,

Hal Kleine, Hi Bithorn) surrendered 22 hits. Dave Williams of Atlanta collected five hits for the winners. Boguskie, Carl Sawatski and Tookie Gilbert (Larry Gilbert's youngest son) were the batting stars for Nashville.

In the July 8, 1953 All-Star game, the Vols jumped on the Stars in the first inning, scoring five runs. The Stars came back in the third inning recording four runs and Vols first baseman Gail Harris clubbed a fourth inning solo home run to give Nashville a 6-4 advantage.

The Stars won it in the sixth when they scored three times on four straight hits and a Vols error for a 7-6 lead. They added an insurance run in the ninth for an 8-6 final. Shortstop Bill Gardner collected three hits for the

Tommy Brown played for the Vols (1955-57) and reached base 20 consecutive times in four games (1956). *Courtesy of The Metropolitan Government Archives of Nashville and Davidson County.*

Vols. The game was played before 7,569 fans at Sulphur Dell.

On July 17, 1957, old Sulphur Dell was host to 7,542 fans on a miserable night with nearly a two-hour rain delay between the second and third innings. Nashville lost to the All-Stars, 7-6 when future Hall of Famer Harmon Killebrew (Chattanooga) doubled in the ninth inning and scored the tie breaking run on a single by Jim McManus.

Vols third baseman, Tommy Brown, was 3-for-5 scoring two runs and belting a home run over the left-field fence. Nashville skipper Dick Sisler used four pitchers who gave up a total of 16 hits. The All-Stars, who never trailed, used five pitchers, allowing Nashville just seven hits on the night.

On July 12, 1979, Nashville's Herschel Greer Stadium hosted the game between the Southern League All-Stars and the Atlanta Braves. Duane Walker of the Nashville Sounds earned MVP honors as the All-Stars beat Atlanta, 5-2. Appearing for the Braves were 1978 Rookie-of-the-Year Bob Horner,

$2.25

1994 Official Souvenir Program

Hershel Greer Stadium hosted the 1994 Triple-A All-Star game where players within three leagues were divided into two teams. *Courtesy of Jeremy Jones.*

Dale Murphy, Glenn Hubbard and former David Lipscomb College pitcher Bo McLaughlin.

Other All-Star participates were Tim Raines (Memphis), Joe Charboneau (Chattanooga) and Dan Heep (Columbus). Also representing the Sounds were Dave Van Gorder, Geoff Combe and Paul Householder.

On June 19, 1983, the defending Southern League champion Sounds played the SL All-Stars at Greer Stadium. A crowd of only 1,221 was in attendance. Nashville, managed by Doug Holmquist, dropped a 3-2 decision to the Stars. The Stars took a 3-0 lead in the sixth inning on singles by Carlos Rios (Savannah) and Butch Davis (Jacksonville) followed by a three-run home run by George Foussianes (Birmingham). Foussianes was the game's MVP. Major League Baseball Commissioner Bowie Kuhn threw out the first pitch.

The Sounds rallied for two runs in the eighth on singles by Frank Kneuer and Pete Dalena and a walk to Erik Peterson loaded the bases. Scott Bradley hit a single to center scoring Kneuer. Derwin McNealy scored the second run on a groundout.

Triple-A Minor League baseball held a joint All-Star game in Greer Stadium on July 13, 1994. All-Star players within the American Association, International and Pacific Coast Leagues were divided between their National and American League affiliates. The Nashville Sounds were affiliated with the Chicago White Sox at this time. The Nationals beat the Americans, 8-5 in front of 11,601 fans. Representing the Sounds were Ray Durham, Drew Denson and Steve Schrenk. Durham was selected as the "Star-of-Stars" of the American Association.

Baseball's Legends Play in Nashville

As Nashville fielded professional baseball clubs since 1885, the city would attract major league teams on their northern journey home from spring training sites in the South for exhibition games. Most games involved the Nashville teams or an opposing major league club.

Some of the greatest baseball players ever to don a major league uniform displayed their extraordinary talents in Nashville. These games were meaningless as far as determining a place in the standings, but to Nashville fans the presence of these skillful players gave memories that lasted forever. Many teams and players appeared more than once especially in the Sulphur Dell ballpark. In documenting a portion of these players the year of their Hall of Fame induction is in parentheses.

During the early spring in 1885, the Chicago White Stockings called Nashville home for its three-week spring training site. Cap Anson was the Chicago player/manager and the premier hitter in the National League at the time. Anson, playing first base for the White Stockings, appeared in several exhibition games against the Nashville Americans.

Also making an appearance with the Chicago club was their star pitcher John Clarkson (1963). Clarkson was an amazing 53-16 in 1885 in this era of two-man rotations. Anson was inducted into the National Baseball Hall of Fame in 1939. Playing in right field for Chicago was Michael "King" Kelly (1945).

In 1887, the Detroit Wolverines played a two-game series with the Nashville Blues. Detroit first baseman Dan Brouthers (1945) began his career in 1879 and retired in 1904. He won five batting titles with a career batting average of .342, which ranks the ninth highest in major league history. His teammate Sam Thompson (1974), known throughout the baseball world as "Big Sam," led the National League in 1887 in batting (.372), hits (203) and RBIs (166).

In 1893, the famous Baltimore Orioles came to our city for an exhibition game with the Nashville Tigers. John McGraw (1937) was the O's short-stop earning the name "Little Napoleon." The left-handed batter with a .333 career batting average later became a successful manager, collecting three World Series titles (1906, 1921, 1922).

Playing for the Cleveland Spiders in 1895, pitcher Cy Young went the distance in an exhibition loss against the Nashville Seraphs. *Courtesy of the Library of Congress.*

A pair of McGraw's teammates also made it to the HOF. Outfielder Joe Kelley (1971) had his best season in 1894 batting .393 with 167 runs scored (second most in NL history.) Wilbert Robinson (1945) was a catcher playing 17 seasons and a manager for 18 more years. Orioles' manager Ned Hanlon was enshrined in 1996. These Orioles were at the beginning of a dynasty winning National League titles in 1894-1896.

The Cleveland Spiders dropped by Athletic Park for a three-game series with the Nashville Seraphs in 1895. The ace pitcher for the Spiders was Cy Young. Young was in his sixth season with Cleveland and already unbelievable. He recorded these totals in 1891 (27-22), 1892 (36-12), 1893 (34-16) and 1894 (26-21). In his lone Nashville exhibition outing, Young went the distance in a Spiders 4-3 loss giving up nine hits. Young was 3-for-4 as a batter.

Young would lead the NL with a 35-10 record in 1895. In his 22 seasons, mostly as a Red Sox player, Young pitched for an astonishing 511-315 record. His wins and loss totals are major league records. He appeared in 906 career games with a 2.63 ERA, five 30-win seasons, 750 complete games and 76 shutouts. Young was selected for the Hall of Fame in 1937. Also playing in the series were teammates Jesse Burkett (1946) and Bobby Wallace (1953).

In March 1905, John McGraw (1937) was back in Nashville as the manager of the reigning NL champions New York Giants. His pair of pitching aces included Christy Mathewson and Joe McGinnity (1946). The Nashville Vols were their opponents in a doubleheader at Athletic Park. The visitors were victorious in both games.

Mathewson won the first game 13-2, while McGinnity took the victory in the five-inning nightcap, 4-0. The Giants would repeat as pennant winners in 1905 and defeat the Philadelphia A's in the World Series. Mathewson was 31-8 with a 1.27 ERA and McGinnity was 21-15 for the season. Mathewson was selected to the Hall of Fame in 1936 as a charter member.

Honus Wagner's Pittsburgh Pirates came to Nashville in 1906 to play the Vols in a two-game series on the University of Nashville's Peabody Field. In the role of player/manager for the Pirates was Fred Clarke (1945). Wagner was

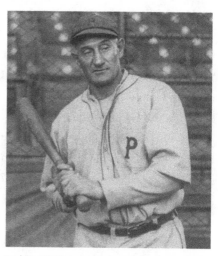

In his **1906 appearances against Nashville, Honus Wagner played in two games on the University of Nashville's Peabody Field.** *Courtesy of the National Baseball Hall of Fame and Library, Cooperstown, New York.*

3-for-4 in the first game with a double and two singles. Clarke slugged the only home run of the game, which the Pirates won, 10-0.

Pittsburgh lost the second game to Nashville, 3-1. Wagner was hitless on the day. The shortstop led the NL in 1906 in batting (.339). "The Flying Dutchman" was enshrined as a charter member of the Hall of Fame in 1936.

For his career, Wagner batted .327 with 3,418 hits, while batting over .300 in 15 consecutive seasons (1899-1913).

In 1909, the most famous double play combination in baseball history of "Evers to Tinker to Chance" arrived at Sulphur Dell for an exhibition contest. The trio was representing the Chicago Cubs. Johnny Evers would play 18 seasons in 1,783 games, batting .270 with 70 triples.

Joe Tinker was the Cubs regular shortstop for 11 seasons and a player/manager in 1913-16. Tinker's career fielding average was .938. First baseman Frank Chance was a Cub from 1898-1914 appearing in 1,286 games with a career fielding percentage of .984. This historic threesome went into the Hall of Fame together in 1946.

The famed manager Connie Mack led his Philadelphia Athletics to Nashville in 1913 for an exhibition with the Vols. In the A's lineup were Frank "Home Run" Baker (1955) and Eddie Collins (1939). Each clubbed a home run with Collins coming by way of an inside the park variety with the bases loaded in the A's 11-8 victory.

Mack began his managerial career in 1894 with the Pittsburgh Pirates. He moved to Philadelphia in 1901 and remained there until 1950. In an amazing 53 years, Mack won a record 3,371 games while losing 3,984. Mack's teams appeared in eight World Series, winning five. He was enshrined into the Hall of Fame in 1937.

In September 1914, Rube Foster (1981) brought his Chicago American Giants, one of the greatest black baseball clubs ever assembled, to Sulphur Dell. Foster was a pioneer in black baseball as a pitcher, manager, executive, promoter and league founder. In Nashville, he pitched against an All-Star team formed from the Nashville Capital City League. During his career (1902-26), Foster played for several teams and organized the first black baseball league in 1920, the Negro National League serving as president and treasurer.

In 1914, the Boston Red Sox battled the Vols on the Vanderbilt University campus. Leading the way for the Sox was Tris Speaker, who in the first inning slugged a two-run home run "over the bunch of trees behind the right field seats." A Nashville newspaper reported that it was the longest ball ever hit on the original Dudley Field.

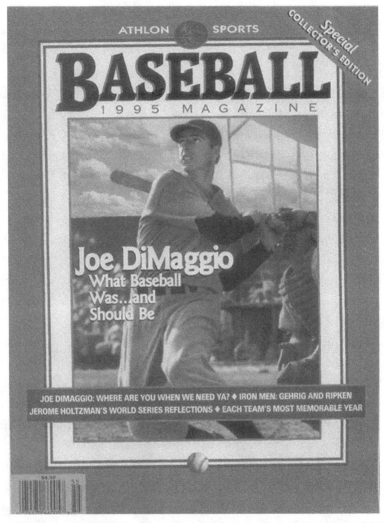

Joe DiMaggio collected a double and a pair of singles in a 1942 spring exhibition game against the Vols. *Courtesy of the author.*

Speaker was selected for the Hall of Fame in 1937 after playing with the Red Sox (1907-15), Cleveland (1916-26), Washington (1927) and Athletics (1928). The centerfielder batted .344 for a career in 2,789 games with 117 home runs and 1,559 RBI's. Also appearing for the Boston in Nashville that April afternoon was rightfielder Harry Hooper (1971).

Babe Ruth and the New York Yankees made many trips to Nashville in the 1920's and 1930's. One of those great Yankees' team came to Nashville in 1927 to face the St. Louis Cardinals at Sulphur Dell for an exhibition. Numerous future Hall of Famers made an appearance: Babe Ruth (1936), Lou Gehrig (1939), Earle Combes (1970), Tony Lazzeri (1991), Waite Hoyt (1969) and manager Miller Huggins (1964).

The Cardinals, 10-8 winners, were represented into the HOF by Grover Cleveland Alexander (1938) who did not play, Jim Bottomley (1974), Frankie Frisch (1947) and Chuck Hafey (1971). Ruth and Frisch each hit home runs in the game.

In 1928, the Nashville Vols were matched with the Boston Braves who was led by second baseman Rogers Hornsby (1942). The Braves routed the Vols 13-3, with Hornsby going 3-for-5 in the game. Only Ty Cobb had a higher career batting average than Hornsby's lifetime .358. Hornsby played his best baseball for the St. Louis Cardinals (1915-26). He was a manager for 14 seasons.

On an April afternoon in 1942, Nashvillians took a break from the war news to witness Joe DiMaggio (1955) leading the Yankees in a two-game series against Nashville. The "Yankee Clipper" collected a double and a pair of singles in an 11-6 Yanks game one win. Additional Yankees' Hall of Famers appearing were Lefty Gomez (1972), Bill Dickey (1964), Red Ruffing (1967), Phil Rizzuto (1994) and manager Joe McCarthy (1957).

McCarthy was back in Nashville in 1950 as the manager of the Boston Red Sox. His star player this trip was Ted Williams (1966). In the exhibition with the Vols, "The Splendid Splinter" recorded one single in the Sox's 7-5 victory. Williams was an 18-time All-Star, six-time batting champion and four-time home run champ. Boston second baseman Bobby Doerr (1986) also played in the game.

The popular Yankees were back in the spring of 1953 for a contest with the Vols. Legendary manager Casey Stengel (1966) led his defending World Series champions with a youthful center-fielding slugger Mickey Mantle (1974). The switch-hitter recorded a double in a 1-for-4 day in the "Bronx Bombers" 9-1 rout.

Mantle participated in 12 World Series (seven championships) and holds WS records for most home runs (18), RBI's (40), runs (42) and hits (26). Behind the plate for the Yanks was Yogi Berra (1972) who collected a single. Johnny Mize (1981) recorded a sacrifice fly to drive in a run.

The Brooklyn Dodgers changed the game of baseball with the signing of Jackie Robinson in 1945. Baseball's first black player made an appearance in Sulphur Dell with an exhibition with the Milwaukee Braves in 1953. The Dodgers defeated the Braves, 3-1 while Robinson recorded two singles.

While Robinson received his Hall of Fame plaque in 1962, teammates Duke Snider (1980), Pee Wee Reese (1984) and Roy Campanella (1969) would also be immortalized in Cooperstown. Opposing these "Bums" were Braves' Hall of Famers Eddie Mathews (1978) and Warren Spahn (1973). Spahn was the losing pitcher in the Nashville exhibition.

In 1955, the Braves and Dodgers played an exhibition in Sulphur Dell. Braves rookie leftfielder Henry Aaron (1982) hit a first inning two-run homer over the left-field fence. Aaron clubbed 755 career homes runs to pass Babe Ruth's 714. Brooklyn manager Walter Alston (1983) was in his second year lead-

In 1955, Milwaukee Braves outfielder Henry Aaron clubbed a first inning, two-run homer in a game against Brooklyn in Sulphur Dell. *Courtesy of the author.*

ing the Dodgers. Alston (1954-76) won four World Series (1955, 1959, 1963, 1965).

Also appearing in Brooklyn's 10-8 victory was Tom Lasorda (1997) who pitched in relief. Lasorda was a pitcher in the Dodgers organization and would later manage the Los Angeles Dodgers for 20 years (1977-1996).

In 1960, Sulphur Dell hosted the Milwaukee Braves versus the Cincinnati Reds. Hank Aaron (1982) collected one hit in two at-bats as the Braves won 6-3. Spahn pitched four innings for the Braves while Mathews (1978) and Red Schoendienst (1989) made appearances. Frank Robinson (1982) played left field for the Reds, securing one hit and a RBI.

Professional baseball left Nashville in 1963 and Sulphur Dell was demolished in 1969. But, the National Pastime returned in 1978 with the Nashville Sounds playing in Herschel Greer Stadium. The Sounds greeted their parent club the New York Yankees in 1981 and 1983. The big guns for New York were Reggie Jackson (1993) and Dave Winfield (2001). The pinstripers routed the Sounds, 10-1. Jackson was 2-for-5 with a double, single and four RBI's, while Winfield added a single.

Several additional exhibition games have been played at Greer that included these future Hall of Famers: Carlton Fisk (2000), Ozzie Smith (2002), Eddie Murray (2003), Goose Gossage (2008), Barry Larkin (2012), Frank Thomas (2014) and managers Tony LaRussa (2014) and Bobby Cox (2014).

LBJ Tosses Ceremonial First Pitch

The Nashville Vols were honored to have Vice President Lyndon Johnson throw out the ceremonial first pitch of its April 8, 1961 opening day at Sulphur Dell. Newspaper accounts indicated the Sulphur Dell toss was the first by a vice-president on an opening day at a minor league park.

Johnson, in office less than three months after the election of President John F. Kennedy, arrived in Nashville from Washington D.C., after an extended trip to Europe and Africa. The vice president was the invited guest speaker at the Jefferson/Jackson Day dinner at the Nashville Fairgrounds Coliseum.

Other dignitaries to accompany Johnson were Sen. Albert Gore Sr., Sen. Estes Kefauver, Rep. J. Carlton Loser, Governor Buford Ellington and Mayor Ben West. After arriving at the airport on an American Airlines commercial flight, Johnson was provided with a police escort to downtown Nashville for the starting point of a parade.

Leading the parade to the final destination at the Sulphur Dell ballpark was the Isaac Litton High School's 130-piece marching band. Also appearing in the parade were certain units of the Al Menah Shrine, former Nashville major league baseball players Johnny Beazley and Clydell Castleman and members of the Nashville Vols.

Prior to the 2:30 afternoon game, Ellington presented to Johnson as a gift a four-year-old Tennessee Walking Horse. The horse was purchased by several Walking Horse enthusiasts and renamed "The Vice-President's Lady."

Johnson later changed the name of the former show horse to "Lady B" after his wife. The horse died in the mid-1980s and is buried on the LBJ ranch. The horse outlived LBJ who died in 1973.

On April 8, 1961, Vice-President Lyndon Johnson threw out the ceremonial first pitch in the Nashville Vols opener at Sulphur Dell. *Courtesy of the Lyndon Baines Johnson Presidential Library.*

"I am an enthusiastic sports fan," Johnson said upon his arrival at the ballpark, "baseball is my favorite game."

Showing his political skills in not offending any baseball fans, Johnson refused to reveal his favorite major league baseball team when asked. He did say that the Austin Senators were probably his favorite baseball team. The Texan also said his favorite baseball players were Babe Ruth, Walter Johnson and Pete Runnels.

"I was just an average player," Johnson said about playing high school baseball in Austin, Texas. "They had me at first base since I was the tallest on the team, but you might say that I was good field, no hit, and not even too good in the field."

When Johnson approached the pitching mound for the ceremonial first pitch, waiting for him at home plate were West, Loser, Ellington and clowns. Loser was positioned behind the plate as a catcher; Ellington was acting as umpire while West stood up to the plate with a bat in hand. Al Menah Shrine clowns were cheerleaders.

The fans greeted Johnson and Ellington with a warm welcome, but it was reported that West and Loser were met with a few boos.

Johnson's throw was wild as West had to do a little dance to get out of the way. The Vice-President said his arm was not in shape to pitch a game. Johnson then addressed the 5,200 fans in the stands.

"I learned early in my political career never to make a speech at a country dance or sports event, and I don't intend to make one here," Johnson said.

"I am proud to be in a state that has produced such great statesmen, and beautiful horses. Your Governor Ellington is one of the finest statesmen in the land. I would like to thank you all from the bottom of a grateful heart."

Just as Johnson spoke his final word, a spectator in the stands shouted, "Play ball!" The game between Nashville and Chattanooga began with Johnson leaving the ballpark after the Lookouts batted in the first inning. The Vols would eventually lose to the Lookouts, 5-3.

The Johnson party was then led to the State Capital Building for a news conference where he answered political questions. Johnson was presented with a pair of cowboy boots monogrammed with "LBJ," a gift that was manufactured at the Cookeville Acme Boot Co.

Later that evening, Johnson gave his speech at the fairgrounds dinner. A few days later, Johnson was in Washington where he joined Kennedy, who opened the major league season with his ceremonial first pitch at Griffith Stadium. Johnson became president in November, 1963 with the death of Kennedy. He would be elected on his own right the following year.

Attending the special event were (left to right) Congressman Carlton Loser, LBJ, Tennessee Governor Buford Ellington and Nashville Mayor Ben West. *Courtesy of the Lyndon Baines Johnson Library.*

In 1965, Johnson became the first president to dedicate a new ballpark. During an exhibition game he opened Houston's Astrodome in his home state. Johnson was scheduled to throw out the first pitch, but he arrived late.

Other major league games in which Johnson threw out the first pitch were all in Washington. These games were also on opening day in 1964, 1965 and 1967.

The first president to attend a major league game was Benjamin Harrison. On June 6, 1892, he witnessed Cincinnati defeat Washington, 7-4. Harrison served as president from 1889 to 1893.

William Howard Taft was the first president to throw out the ceremonial first pitch at a baseball game in 1910. The game was on opening day of the season with the Philadelphia Athletics playing at Washington. It was also at this game that during the seventh inning Taft stood to stretch. This is where the "seventh inning stretch" was believed to have originated.

A meeting between President Calvin Coolidge and Babe Ruth occurred when the New York Yankees arrived in Washington one day to play the Senators. The weather was on Ruth's mind as he extended his hand to the president and said, "Hot as hell, ain't it, Prez?"

Vols Say Good-Bye in 1963

The Sulphur Dell ballpark was known for its strange dimensions, due to the configuration of the city block where it was constructed. There was a 45-degree embankment around the entire outfield that was part of the playing field. The outfield fence, 16 feet high, was on top of the embankment. The right field fence was only 262 feet from home plate and the bottom of the fence was 22½ feet above the playing field. Left field was 334 feet and center field 421 feet from home plate. On top of the fence was a screen that measured 30 feet in height in left and right field, decreasing to 22½ feet midway to center field. The playing field itself was below street level and would frequently flood during heavy rains due to its proximity to Cumberland River.

Nashville sports writer Grantland Rice renamed the park (known at the time as Athletic Park) Sulphur Dell mostly for the nearby sulphur spring and "dell" was easier for rhyming in his poetic style stories. In 1927, the grandstands were demolished and rebuilt with the playing field facing the opposite direction. Opposing ball players would refer to the ballpark as "Suffer Hell." And the treacherous right field was referred to as the "Dump."

During the 1950s, attendance for the Southern Association's members was on the decline. From a high in 1947 of 2,180,344 to a low of 780,316 in 1960, the association's officials watched attendance fall dramatically.

In 1960, New Orleans, charter member in 1901, gave up its franchise when low attendance forced the Pelicans out of the association. Also, before the 1960 season began, Memphis' ballpark burned to the ground, forcing the Chicks to play baseball in two municipal parks. They drew only 48,487 fans, an average of 600 per game. The Chicks folded at the end of that season.

The situation became worse in 1961, with only 647,831 fans attending Southern Association games, an average of 1,000 per game. The Southern

At one time Sulphur Dell was known as "Baseball's Most Historic Park Since 1970." Notice the rightfielder standing on top of the 45-degree embankment that extended along the outfield. *Courtesy of the Metropolitan Archives of Nashville and Davidson County.*

Association could not support itself, and after 61 years, the circuit folded. The Nashville Vols had not won a pennant since 1949 and was a team without a league.

The Sulphur Dell ballpark would not be silent in 1962 as it hosted local high school, amateur, junior league, barnstorming games and non-sporting events. In 1963, the Nashville Vols had re-emerged by joining old Southern Association rivals Chattanooga and Macon in the South Atlantic League (SALLY). In 1959, the Nashville Vols became a corporation formed by 4,876 stockholders (Vols, Inc.) who were baseball fans. A Board of Trust overlooked the team's operation.

The 1963 attendance in Nashville was dismal. During the season, rumors and speculation were circulating that professional baseball in Nashville would no longer exist after the year. The Vols' last game at Sulphur Dell was a doubleheader played on September 8 against Lynchburg. The Vols won both games, 6-3 and 2-1.

This centerfielder's view of the Sulphur Dell grandstand is from a 1953 scorecard. *Courtesy of the author.*

Nashville rightfielder, Charlie Teuscher, clubbed three home runs on the day. He hit a three-run shot in the opening game and a walk-off solo blast in the eighth inning of the nightcap that went into extra innings. It had been announced before the final scheduled games at Sulphur Dell that a meeting would be held within the Board of Trust to determine the final fate of the fan-owned Vols. The few fans that attended both season-ending games were wondering if they were enjoying the final contests in Nashville.

Sports writer Raymond Johnson of the *Tennessean* wrote in his column:

They came not to praise Caesar, but to bury him. They were not Shakespearean fans, those 971 who came to Sulphur Dell yesterday to pay their last respects to the Nashville Vols. They were dyed-in-the-wool lovers of baseball who came to see the farewell game in the nation's most historic park.

They went away praising the Vols for a fine afternoon's performance, climaxed by Charlie Teuscher's home run, the blow which gave Southern League pitchers nightmares for more than 60 years. Charlie's drive, his third out-of-the-park for the day, gave the Vols a double victory for the faithful fans' memoirs.

These fans, most of them fearing the worst but hoping something will turn up to enable baseball to continue here, came from many surrounding towns. Quite a few of the spectators have been watching games in the Dell for half a century.

It was a day well worth driving more than 100 miles to get here. Talking with countless fans, all of them with the same hope, and seeing the 971 stand for perhaps 30 seconds when Teuscher homered before making a move to leave. Like me, they wondered if they would ever see a home run in Sulphur Dell again.

After the Board's September meeting, a decision was made that the Nashville Vols should surrender its franchise in the South Atlantic League. The meeting was held at the Third National Bank with all 27 directors agreeing to the decision. They voted to leave the decision up to the stockholders, Vols, Inc., on whether to dispose of Sulphur Dell and the corporation.

It was reported that the corporation owed $22,000 after all the yearly income and expenses were calculated. The Vols did not have any cash assets. In 1965, country singer Faron Young formed a partnership to bring auto racing to Sulphur Dell. That enterprise lasted a few weeks and Sulphur Dell Speedways was soon out of business.

These original Sulphur Dell ballpark seats are on permanent display at the Metropolitan Government Archives of Nashville and Davidson County. *Courtesy of the author.*

F.M. Williams wrote this story in 1969 about the demolition of Sulphur Dell:

About 35 people with a million memories said goodbye to Sulphur Dell yesterday. Shortly after 2 p.m., a giant claw was raised to the grandstand roof near the rightfielder fence and took a giant bite out of one of Nashville's best-known landmarks.

Within six to eight weeks, all that remains of what once was the nation's oldest baseball park will have vanished, the victim of the city's rapidly changing skyline. In its place, within the year, hopefully, will raise a $4 to $5 million 18-story merchandising mart. Gregg Industries, Inc., which bought the Dell from almost 5,000 baseball fans a few months ago for $255,00, will build the mart.

But for the few who bothered to pay a last visit to the Dell, today and tomorrow gave way to yesterday, and its many memories of victory and defeat.

The mart project never materialized and the State of Tennessee eventually acquired the land, which became a parking lot. Of the 35 people attending the first day demolition was Mrs. Jim Turner, the wife of former New York Yankee pitching coach and manager of the Vols in 1960. Mrs. Turner brought her home movie camera and took plenty of film of the worn out ballpark before the wrecking ball went to work.

Nashville would again acquire a minor league team in 1978 with the Double-A Nashville Sounds of the Southern League. A new ballpark was built and named for Herschel Greer, an avid baseball fan and supporter of Nashville youth baseball. Greer was one of the organizers of Vols, Inc. and headed the drive to sell stock in an effort to keep baseball in Nashville.

PART III

Nashville Sounds:
The Tradition Grows

The Nashville Sounds' First Season

On September 8, 1963, the Nashville Vols entered into a season-ending, seven-inning doubleheader with Lynchburg. The Vols won the first game 6-3 while the second game was tied 1-1 going into extra innings.

Nashville Vols batter Charlie Teuscher would lead off the last of the eighth inning. Teuscher, after showing his anguish on a called strike by the umpire, promptly lifted the next pitch over the famous short right field screen. The home run would end the game, and though it was not known at the time, ended professional baseball in Nashville.

Only an average of 921 fans attended the games that season, bringing the season total to a mere 54,435. This was the lowest total in the 103-year history of the Vols. Rumors persisted all season long that this could be the final season for the Vols. The Sulphur Dell ballpark had been empty during the 1962 season then Nashville joined the Sally League in 1963. Sulphur Dell, the oldest ballpark in the country, was demolished in 1969.

It would be 15 years before professional baseball returned to Nashville. In 1978, the Nashville Sounds came into existence. This was due to the force of Vanderbilt head baseball coach Larry Schmittou, who became president and majority owner of the Sounds. Former David Lipscomb baseball player Farrell Owens was the general manager and part owner. Other part owners were Conway Twitty, Jerry Reed, Walter Nipper, Bob Elliott, Billy Griggs, Jimmy Miller, Cal Smith, Gene Smith, Marcella Smith, Reese Smith, Jr, Reese Smith III, Steven Smith and L.E. White.

The new home for the Sounds was Herschel Greer Stadium, constructed at the base of St. Cloud Hill in Fort Negley Park, a former Union Army encampment during the Civil War. The first year seating capacity was

This is the Nashville Sounds first official souvenir program. *Courtesy of the author.*

7,200, with plans for an additional 2,000 seats the next year. It was named for Herschel Lynn Greer, a longtime supporter of Nashville's amateur baseball and one-time president of Nashville Vols, Inc. The site, owned by the Nashville Metro Government, had consisted of four softball fields and a fenced baseball field for youth leagues.

The Sounds were members of the Double-A Southern League and the major league affiliate of the Cincinnati Reds. The Sounds were assigned to the Western Division with Knoxville, Memphis, Chattanooga and Montgomery. Eastern Division teams were Columbus, Jacksonville, Orlando, Savannah and Charlotte. The previous year the franchise was located in Three Rivers (Canada), also Double-A.

The Sounds played their momentous first game on April 15, 1978 in Memphis. The game was played in Tim McCarver Stadium, home of the Memphis Chicks. Nearly 9,200 fans jammed into the 5,500-seat stadium for opening day.

Chuck Goggin was the Sounds manager and his first lineup included: Steve Hughes, SS; Randy Davidson, 2B; Don Lyle, DH; Tim Doerr, 3B; George Weicker, 1B; Tony Moretto, RF; Mickey Duval, CF; Mark Miller, C; Duane Walker, RF and Bill Dawley, P.

The Memphis fans were happy as their Chicks defeated the Sounds, 4-2. Nashville fell behind 1-0 after the opening inning, but tied the game in the third on Duval's RBI double scoring Hughes. In the sixth frame, Weicker delivered a single plating Duval for a Sounds 2-1 lead.

Memphis rallied for three unearned runs in their half of the sixth with their bullpen shutting out the Sounds to close the game. Dawley took the loss for the Sounds, while former Vanderbilt pitcher Scott Sanderson, in his second season of professional baseball, secured the Chicks victory. The 9,197 fans broke a Memphis attendance record.

The next day, behind the strong pitching of starter Bruce Berenyi and reliever Doug Corbett, Nashville shutout the Chicks, 3-0. Berenyi pitched the first six innings, recording three hits and eight strikeouts while walking one batter. Corbett retired nine straight batters, including four K's, to pick up a save. The historic victory gave the Sounds their first win before 2,465 Memphis fans.

In the third inning, the Sounds scored two runs off an RBI double by Miller and a sacrifice fly by Davidson. The final tally came in the fifth on a Moretto double. Miller and Lyle each recorded two of the Sounds total nine hits. In 17 innings the Sounds' pitching had allowed just one earned run.

Chuck Goggin was the Sounds' first manager and a Vietnam veteran, with major league experience with Pittsburgh and Atlanta. *Courtesy of the Nashville Sounds.*

The Sounds returned to Nashville for their inaugural home game on April 26 to face the Savannah Braves. They entered the game in third place behind Knoxville and Memphis, with a 5-4 record. An overflowing crowd of 8,156 witnessed the historic night. The originally scheduled opening game was rained out the previous night. Also making their first appearance were the lovely "Soundettes" who assisted the fans.

It was considered a miracle that the field was ready for play. The team requested to open the season on the road and had to swap a series with Chattanooga in order to have enough time to complete the stadium and the field. Even though the Sounds opened the season on the road, Greer Stadium was not ready. The sod had been laid the day before, thanks to 50 fans that volunteered to lay the sod for a "sod party." And on game day tractors and grading machines were still at work.

The home faithful were not disappointed. Joe Griffin led a 16-hit Sounds outburst driving in five runs with four hits in a Sounds 12-4 victory. Moretto and Duval added three hits apiece for the Sounds. Berenyi picked up the win after pitching five innings. Larry Rothschild gave up three runs in a third of an inning for the Sounds. Corbett came on to retire eleven Braves in a row to record the save.

"The field was playable although it was not 100 percent," Goggin said after the game. "I think Savannah got a couple of bad hops and we took advantage of them. We were really fired up and swinging the bats."

Southern League President Billy Hitchcock was on hand to welcome baseball back to the Music City. The start of the game was delayed for 30 minutes due to traffic problems at the stadium.

Herschel Greer Stadium opened its gates for the first time in 1978 and hosted its last game in 2014 as First Tennessee Park was being constructed. *Courtesy of the Nashville Sounds.*

"After seeing the baseball stadium in the condition it was in when we got here late Monday night, it's amazing, really incredible that it was in such good condition on the infield," said Sounds second baseman Randy Davidson. "That grounds crew did a super job getting the sod down. The fans were really sensational, and I'm glad we could win this one for them. I hope it brings them back."

It was reported that the concession and souvenir stands were virtually sold out by the time the game was over at 11 pm. William Lazenby and his 16-year-old son Robert were credited with being the first paying fans through the turnstile. The Sounds finished the season with a 64-77 record in ninth place of the league standings.

"I used to spend a lot of time watching the old Vols play down at Sulphur Dell," said Lazenby. "I've been waiting ever since that last Vol's game for the day that this kind of entertainment came back to Nashville, and I'm glad the wait is over. I used to play on a church league softball team and we had our games down here at Ft. Negley. I even remember when they built the Ft. Negley Park. I've been out here every night since they started building this park to watch how it went along."

This ticket is from the Sounds first game indicating "Game No. 2" since the original home opener was rained out. *Courtesy of the author.*

Sonny Fulks was the plate umpire for that first home game, with his associate, Mike Benda, covering the rest of the field. The Nashville Sounds first radio broadcasters were Monte Hale and Jay Colley, with Ty Coppinger providing the color commentary. Chuck Morgan was the Sounds first stadium PA announcer. In 1978, the Sounds led all of minor league baseball with an attendance of 380,159 fans.

Some called Schmittou a genius for his marketing of the ball club, especially with the promotion nights for the 57 home dates. His goal was to make baseball a family affair and something that was clean and wholesome for everyone. Said Schmittou, "I was convinced, and I'm still convinced, that the people of Nashville were missing something without having a pro baseball team. I was determined to do something about it."

One popular night was guaranteed "Victory Night," in which a fan's ticket was good for the next night if the Sounds won. Fans seemed to give more vocal encouragement rooting their Sounds to victory on these nights. Other minor league teams gave free tickets to their fans if they lost a game.

"I didn't want that," said Schmittou. "You would have people rooting against the home team."

Other promotional nights in that that first season were: Family Night (entire family admitted for $5); Pennant Night; Ball Day, Bat Night; Helmet Night, Used Car Night; All Faith Night; Old Timer's Night; Celebrity Softball games; Senior Citizens Night; Junior Sounds Night; Jacket Night; Fireworks Night, T-Shirt Night and many more.

Concession prices in 1978 included: hot dog (55 cents); hamburger (75 cents); Big Red Smokey (60 cents); one-quarter pounder (95 cents); french fries (40 cents); pizza slice (65 cents); soft drinks (25/35/60 cents); draft beer (55 cents); coffee (25 cents); ice cream (60 cents) peanuts (30 cents); popcorn (30/35 cents) and a candy bar (25 cents).

Larry Schmittou and Nashville Baseball

This Q & A between former Nashville Sounds owner Larry Schmittou and Bill Traughber are from 2008.

Larry Schmittou was born in 1939, and grew up in West Nashville where he graduated from Cohn High School and later George Peabody College. Schmittou coached sandlot baseball throughout the city and would eventually change the landscape of Vanderbilt baseball with his arrival in 1968.

In 1971, the Commodores won their first of four consecutive SEC East titles. In 1973 and the following season, Vanderbilt captured the SEC championship and Schmittou was named SEC Coach of the Year both times. He coached 20 All-SEC players while 124 were taken in the major league drafts. Schmittou is currently ranked third all-time in Vanderbilt wins with a mark of 306-252-1. He trails Roy Mewborne and Tim Corbin.

Schmittou's vision to bring professional baseball back to Nashville was realized in 1978 with the Double-A Nashville Sounds of the Southern League and Herschel Greer Stadium.

During that first season, the Sounds drew 380, 159 fans to lead the league in attendance. In recognition of his achievements, Schmittou was named *Sporting News* Double-A and Southern League Executive-of-the-Year in 1978 and 1981 and the Triple-A *Sporting News* Executive-of-the-Year in 1989.

Bill Traughber: When did you acquire a love for baseball?

Larry Schmittou: I can't remember not having one. I grew up listening to the old Nashville Vols on the radio. Every now and then, usually on a Sunday, my mother would take me down to watch a game at Sulphur Dell. We didn't have a car, but buses ran out to where we lived. Baseball was the sport—period—when I grew up in the late 40's and 50's.

The groundbreaking ceremony for Herschel Greer Stadium. Left to right: Charles Spears, Dick Sisler, Jim Turner, David Scobey (with baseball bat), Charles Caldwell, Larry Schmittou, Lynn Greer and Nashville Mayor Richard Fulton (with shovel). *Courtesy of Larry Schmittou.*

BT: Wasn't there a conflict with you coaching at Vanderbilt and being involved with a professional baseball team?

Schmittou: I coached Vanderbilt the first year we had the Sounds. Then I purchased Greensboro and I wanted to finish coaching Vanderbilt in 1979. I had to appear before the NCAA Executive Committee to get permission because I was involved with pro sports. I just wanted to finish out the year. I made my pitch, but they voted "no" and said I needed to resign then. I resigned in February 1979.

BT: Tell me the demands of setting up professional baseball team in a city without a proper stadium?

Schmittou: My terms with the city was I could lease the land, but have to build the stadium and pay property taxes if we owned the stadium. We had to build that park with our own money. If it not been for Conway Twitty, I could not have put the group together. I had absolutely no money. The bank agreed to loan me $30,000. We thought the stadium was going to cost between $300,000 and $500,000. It ended up costing over a million dollars. I had to go around to beg and borrow to get people to donate products for construction. I had to mortgage my house.

Then the bad weather set in. We had requested to open our schedule on the road. We knew we couldn't get finished before the first home stand. So I needed to get Chattanooga to swap a series with me. They charged me some money to do that. Then tragically for me, a few days before we were supposed to open, my mother passed away. That was weighing on my mind. The sod came in late. We didn't know if we were going to get it down in time. Farrell Owens called a bunch of radio stations to tell them we were going to have a "sod party." Come on out and help us lay sod.

We must have had 50 people come out while some people worked almost all night helping lay and rolling sod. It wasn't in that good of shape. The first game was rained out, but when we did open, it was in front of a full house. The electricity was turned on five minutes before the gates opened.

BT: Cincinnati was your first major league affiliate. You had a disagreement involving the designated hitter rule. Did that hurt your relationship with the Reds?

Schmittou: Chief Bender was the farm director and at first they let us use the DH. Then Bob Howsam (Reds president) came up to see a series. When he went back, he told Chief we could no longer use the DH. They wanted their minor league pitchers to bat since they would have to hit in the National League. We had a decent team that year. When they decided that, I made the announcement that if we couldn't use the DH when the other teams were using the DH, then I wasn't going to renew with them.

I knew that everybody in the world wanted to come to Nashville. I would have no difficulty getting my choice who to sign with. Once they saw we had a new park, people starting calling me to get into the Southern League especially for those with eastern teams where they had bad weather.

BT: With the close relationship you had with the Reds, you must have met some of their former great players.

Larry Schmittou greets Sounds' fans during the 1978 season. *Courtesy of Larry Schmittou.*

Schmittou: Pete Rose and I became friends. We became bigger friends when he became the manager of the Reds. He was very personable with the fans. He would call all the time about his players. When they showed those calls, when he was supposedly calling bookies, some of the calls were the Nashville Sounds number.

He called wanting to know how our players did like how did so-and-so pitch. If he had a player on rehab he wanted to know his progress. Actually when Pete opened his restaurant, we gave him the original seats that we owned from old Atlanta Stadium. When he opened his restaurant in Ft. Lauderdale we gave him eight of those.

BT: Then you were able to switch to the New York Yankees organization. What was your relationship like with George Steinbrenner?

Schmittou: They had tried to get me to go to Triple-A when I first started, but I had already made a commitment to the Reds in Double-A. I told the Yankees that I couldn't go back on my word. So when it was evident that we were not going to resign with the Reds, they immediately called us as well as four or five other clubs. Mr. Steinbrenner at the time owned Nashville Bridge Co., and he wanted to come to Nashville for more reasons than his company.

They were so super with us. They gave us those great teams. He'd come to town himself and do things to raise money for charity. He came to town at my request and got roasted and raised money to build the Eye Cornea Transplant over at Vanderbilt, which is named after his wife Joan. He helped raise money for the Old Timers Baseball Association. We had Vanderbilt play Tennessee one time in my honor and gave them $10,000 to play at Greer Stadium instead of McGugin. He did lots of things for Nashville. Everything I asked of him he did.

BT: Do you have a favorite Steinbrenner memory.

Schmittou: Once he had my whole family sitting up in his box at Yankee Stadium and set us up in a big fancy hotel. We were sitting at a game when Lou Piniella was the manager. The Yankees were getting beat. Mrs. Piniella was in the box with George and us.

Lou made some type of move in the game and George, right in front of everybody, was raving and running Lou down about his decision. About that time my youngest son, Steve, lost a tooth. He was about 10 years old and had a loose tooth. All of a sudden with the game going on, George is on his knees. Mrs. Piniella was on her knees with my wife looking for my son's tooth.

BT: You must have met some of the Yankees' great legends?

Schmittou Mickey Mantle came down with George a lot. Yogi Berra was special. Yogi came down during the strike and spent eight days with us. Yogi is a very intelligent man. He sat in the press box and never took a note. He wanted to talk about life. He didn't talk much about baseball. He did tell some funny stories though.

At the end of those eight days, Yogi went down to address our team. Yogi discussed [Sounds] game-by-game from memory on everything from such-and-such you needed to move so-and-so over in the third inning of the first ball game. If you hit behind the runner, you should have moved him from second to third. I just sat there in amazement. He never wrote down a note. It was all from memory sitting in the press box.

BT: In 1993 and 1994, you brought in a second baseball team, the Nashville Xpress. How did that develop?

Schmittou: There was only one thought. I also owned Huntsville at the time. They were Double-A, and with major league expansion, Charlotte became the affiliate. The man that owned the expansion Double-A team didn't have a place to play. If they didn't find a home, I would have lost 16 home games in Huntsville. Everybody else in the league would have lost 16 home games.

We would have had only nine teams and everybody would have been open four days in a row. Nobody wanted that to happen. I asked my people what they thought about bringing the team to Nashville. They were Gung Ho about it. It was the easiest two years for my staff in all the 19 years. We could have a regular week. Somebody was there every night.

BT: What was the worse part about owning a minor league baseball team?

Sounds owner Larry Schmittou meets with New York Yankees' personnel in the fall of 1979 to sign a working agreement with the team. Left to right: Schmittou, George Steinbrenner, Whitey Ford, Bill White, Mickey Vernon and Bill Bergesch. *Courtesy of Larry Schmittou.*

Schmittou: You can have too many owners and you can have too many politicians and you have too much press.

BT: What is your fondest memory about your experience with the Sounds?

Schmittou: We were able to bring baseball back. It was successful and we stayed there. And we built a nice stadium for its time that has lasted 30 years. It's still a great place to watch a game.

BT: Why did you sell all your financial interest with the Sounds and the other minor league clubs you owned, and leave baseball?

Schmittou: When the Titans came to town, I knew where the money was going. I decided it was time for me to exit and do something else.

BT: With all of the Sounds players you've been connected with, who was your favorite?

Schmittou: Skeeter Barnes. The reason Skeeter is my favorite is he's one that no matter whatever bad happened to him, he still worked the hardest. He had that cheerful face on him. Skeeter came to us in 1979 right out of high school. He wasn't a very good fielder. He bounced around the minors and maybe got called up in September one year. Then he came back to us when we were with the Reds. He was always the first person who was cheerful and inspiring to people.

He would play any position you asked him to. He came in one day after the 1993 season and asked if I'd recommend him for a job on the fire department in Indianapolis where he was from. I told him I'd be happy to, but he was probably making as much money in Double-A and winter ball as he would as a fireman. I told him he should keep playing baseball until he couldn't play anymore.

Fortunately the next year he was with Detroit, got called up and spent four or five years with them. He usually called me every week. His attitude is what made him one of my favorites. Skeeter wasn't the best player, but he worked harder than anybody I saw coming through there.

Schmittou was an owner and president of the Sounds for 19 years (1978-96). He served as vice-president of Marketing for the Texas Rangers from 1983 to 1986, commuting between Nashville and Arlington. Schmittou is currently president of Strike &

Spare Family Fun Center in Hendersonville, TN that operates bowling chains in Tennessee and Kentucky. In 2006, Schmittou was inducted into the Tennessee Sports Hall of Fame and the Vanderbilt Sports Hall of Fame (2016). He was also presented the Fred Russell Lifetime Achievement Award by the Nashville Sports Council (2011) and inducted into the Southern League Hall of Fame (2016).

Nashville Sounds' Championships

Since the Nashville Sounds came into existence in 1978, the team has only managed to win three championships. Nevertheless, in just their second year, manager George Scherger led the Sounds to their first Southern League championship.

The Double-A Sounds (Cincinnati Reds affiliate) finished in second place with an 83-61 record behind Memphis in the Western Division. The Sounds leaped into the championship series by beating Memphis (10-2, 3-4, 5-2) in two-out-of-three games in the first round of the playoffs.

The Sounds were to face the Eastern Division champions Columbus (Ga.) Astros in the best-of-five Southern League championship series. The first game was held at Herschel Greer Stadium before a crowd of 7,100 fans. Nashville pitcher Bill Dawley was working on a perfect game when Columbus' Reggie Baldwin led off the fifth inning with a double.

Reggie Waller singled Baldwin home for the first score of the game. In the seventh inning, Columbus added to their narrow lead when Phil Klimas slugged a two-run home run making the Columbus advantage 3-0. Columbus pitcher Jim McDonald had the Sounds baffled until the home half of the eighth inning. The Sounds used a walk, a double by Tommy Sohns, a Gene Menees single and two Columbus errors to tie the score at 3-3.

In the ninth inning, Kilmas stroked an RBI single to put the visitors ahead, 4-3. The Sounds had a leadoff triple by Rafael Santo Domingo wasted as he was thrown out at the plate on an infield ground ball. Jeff Lahti picked up the loss for the Sounds while McDonald was credited with the victory. Columbus led the series, 1-0.

Game Two was also at Greer Stadium, with Scott Brown pitching for the Sounds and Columbus countering with Ron Meredith. In the third inning, the Astros collected five consecutive hits, but managed only one run. Sounds rightfielder Paul Householder nailed a Columbus runner at the plate with his shotgun arm to kill a potential rally.

In the Sounds third inning, Duane Walker notched a one-out double, scoring Skeeter Barnes and Rick Duncan. Menees followed with a single, scoring Walker and giving the Sounds a 3-1 lead. Geoff Combe relieved Brown in the eighth inning and earned a save in the Sounds 3-1 win. The series was even at 1-1.

The third game of the series moved to Golden Park in Columbus, before only 1,704 fans. Nashville sent pitcher Bill Kelly to the mound who was opposed by Astros' Billy Smith. The Sounds jumped on Smith and Columbus early, scoring seven runs and 10 hits by the third inning.

Sohns hit a three-run home run in the second inning to start the run barrage. Columbus could not rebound and Nashville won the contest, 14-7. Householder walked three times, Walker, Eddie Milner and Barnes recorded three hits apiece. The 17 total hits helped give Nashville a 2-1 edge in the series. Kelly picked up the win.

Game Four of the series remained in Columbus. The Sounds began the scoring in the second inning when Astros' pitcher Del Leatherwood walked

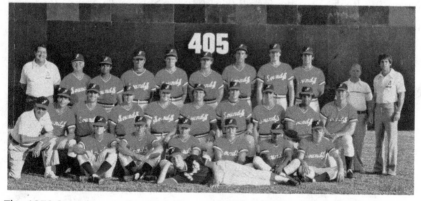

The 1979 Sounds won the city's first professional baseball championship since 1949 winning the Southern League title. *Courtesy of Farrell Owens.*

Barnes. Sohns and Walker followed with successive singles producing the first run. Milner added an RBI single later in the inning putting the Sounds in the lead, 2-0.

Sounds starting pitcher, Randy Town, gave up a run in the fourth inning while the Sounds still led, 2-1. Town ran into trouble in the sixth inning and was relieved by Combe. Combe was the league's most outstanding pitcher that year with a record 30 saves. He did give up a solo home run in the eighth that tied the score at 2-2.

In the ninth inning, the Sounds loaded the bases, and catcher Dave Van Gorder registered a triple to score three runs. The Sounds added one more run in the inning and led 6-2. Combe held on and recorded the win, while Fred Morris took the loss for Columbus. The Nashville Sounds had won their first championship, three games to one.

In 1982, Sounds' skipper Johnny Oates led his ball club to a second-place finish (77-67) behind Memphis. In the first round of the Southern League playoffs the Sounds (Yankees affiliate) defeated Memphis three games to one to advance to the championship series. Their opponent was Jacksonville, winners of the Eastern Division.

The best-of-five championship series opened in Jacksonville's Wolfson Park with Sounds pitcher Sheldon Andrews opposing Suns' pitcher Danny Jackson. In the fourth inning, the Sounds Erik Peterson doubled home Otis Nixon and Buck Showalter for a 2-0 lead. In the Suns fourth inning the home team knotted the score at 2-2 with the aid of three Sounds errors.

In the Suns eighth inning, Jim Atkinson hammered a tie-breaking home run off Sounds reliever Chris Lein. Jacksonville took the opening game 3-2, with Jackson going the distance for the win. Lein took the loss.

In Game Two, the Sounds evened the series at one game each behind the pitching of Ray Fontenot. Fontenot pitched a three-hit complete game while allowing one run in a 4-1 victory.

Brian Dayett drilled a two-run double in the third inning after an RBI single by Nate Chapman. In the Sounds, seventh inning, Peterson doubled home Showalter with the Sounds, final run. Walt Vanderbush took the loss for the Suns.

The third game of the series was played in Greer Stadium before a crowd of 7,316 fans. Sounds ace and Southern League Pitcher-of-the-Year, Stefan Wever, started for the home team. Jacksonville countered with Glenn Ray.

In the first inning, Dayett was robbed of a home run when Suns outfielder Dave Leeper leaped over the wall to snatch the ball, which fell out of his glove to the ground for a double. Showalter, who earlier reached base on an error, scored from second base on the play. Dayett had hit a club record-tying 34 home runs that year and was the league's Most Valuable Player. The Sounds led 1-0 after the first inning.

In the Sounds third inning, Garry Smith hit a double and Ed Rodriguez followed with another two-base hit. The 2-0 lead held as the Sounds won the game to take a 2-1 advantage in the series. Wever's only trouble came in the sixth when the first two Suns reached base. Wever then struck out the next three batters to end the threat.

The Sounds were in a position to win the title before their home fans. Clay Christiansen started for the Sounds. Tim Knight began the scoring in the Sounds second inning with a solo home run. Nashville scored again in the third inning when Nixon walked and stole second. Chapman singled home Nixon for the 2-0 lead.

Dayett scored the Sounds third run as he dashed home from second base on an errant double-play attempt. Christiansen worked seven and

Skipper Johnny Oates led Nashville in 1982 with a 77-67 record and the Southern League crown. *Courtesy of Farrell Owens.*

one-third innings while Nashville took a 3-1 lead into the ninth. Facing the championship loss, Jacksonville tied the game in the ninth with an RBI single by Russ Stephens and a sacrifice fly by Jim Scranton. The Sounds failed to score in their half of the ninth to send the game into extra innings.

The game remained tied 3-3 when the Sounds came to bat in the 13th inning. Dan St. Clair was in relief for Jacksonville. With Showalter on base and two outs, Dayett was the Sounds batter. In front of 4, 106 fans, Dayett smashed a pitch over the double-wall in left centerfielder. The heroic blast gave the Sounds a 5-3 win and their second championship. Guy Elston recorded the win in three innings of relief.

It would be 23 more years until the Sounds would win a league crown. In 2005, Nashville was the Milwaukee Brewers major league affiliate and members of the Triple-A Pacific Coast League. Manager Frank Kremblas led the Sounds to a 75-69 overall record in making the first round of the playoffs. Nashville advanced to the PCL title series defeating Oklahoma in five games.

Game One of the championship series against Tacoma was played at Greer Stadium. The Sounds had an early power surge hitting five of the game's eight home runs. In the Sounds fourth inning, back-to-back-to-back dingers by Tony Zuniga, Nelson Cruz and Mike Rivera gave the home team a 6-5 lead.

Earlier in the game Cruz and Zuniga clubbed home runs for a two-homer night. In the sixth Nashville's Steve Scarborough's RBI double highlighted a two-run inning to eventually give the Sounds an 8-6 victory. Ben Hendrickson started for the Sounds on the mound.

In the second game also played at Greer, an offensive outburst by the Sounds resulted in an 11-5 win. The Sounds scored their first nine runs without a home run until Scarborough led off the eighth inning placing the ball over the fence. Nashville was aided by four Rainers' errors. Sounds starter Tommy Phelps worked six innings to pick up the win while relievers Jeff Housman and Mike Meyers finished the game.

Game Three resulted in a Sounds championship sweep, with a 5-2 win in Tacoma's Cheney Stadium. The Sounds jumped out to a 2-0 lead with a third inning solo home run by Scarborough and a sixth inning RBI single by Rivera. The Rainers picked up two runs in the seventh to tie the game. The contest would go into extra innings with an exciting 13th frame for Nashville.

With two outs, Sounds second baseman Cory Hart reached base on a throwing error by Tacoma's short-stop. With two Sounds on base, Cruz was given the opportunity to become a hero. Cruz clubbed a 1-0 pitch deep over the left field wall for the 5-2 lead. Cruz collected three home runs and 11 RBIs in the series.

Sounds starter Gary Glover worked six and two-thirds innings.

The Sounds won their third championship in 2005 under the leadership of Frank Kremblas for the Pacific Coast League title. *Courtesy of the Nashville Sounds.*

Nashville's bullpen tossed six and one-third scoreless innings. Pitching outstanding baseball in relief were Alec Zumwalt (2.1 innings), Mike Adams (1 inning) and Brett Evert (3 innings). Evert struck out the final Rainers' batter on a check swing to secure the victory.

Buck Showalter's Nashville Years

This exclusive interview between former Sounds' player Buck Showalter and Bill Traughber is from 2011. Showalter is currently the manager of the Baltimore Orioles.

There have been hundreds of players that have appeared in a Nashville Sounds uniform since the club's first season in 1978. Some players advance in the minor league system, move to other franchises, have major league careers or forced out because of injury or lack of ability.

The Sounds have had their share of prominent players to make it to "The Show" and obtain a familiar name in the baseball world. One of these former players to make a name for himself is Buck Showalter. Though Showalter reached Triple-A, he never made it to the major leagues as a player. But he has been a major league manager gaining a reputation for rebuilding struggling teams without strong talent.

Showalter was born in DeFuniak Springs, Fla., and was a First Team All-American in 1977 at Mississippi State. With the Bulldogs, Showalter established a still-standing record batting average (.459). The New York Yankees in the fifth round of the 1977 MLB Amateur Draft selected him. The left-hander played his first three professional seasons in Ft. Lauderdale (Single-A) and West Haven, Conn. (Double-A). Then in 1980, Showalter was in Nashville as a member of the Southern League Sounds (Double-A).

"We had graduated to the big leagues when we came to Nashville," Showalter said recently from his Baltimore Orioles clubhouse office. "You have to understand where we came from. West Haven had one of the worse facilities in minor league baseball. We had two nails for a locker and a piece of tape with your name over it.

"One bathroom with showers was probably the size of most people's garage. It all had to do with Mr. [George] Steinbrenner. He had purchased the Yankees a few years earlier. When he came to West Haven and saw the facility, he immediately wanted an upgrade. There was also the attendance factor playing in Nashville in front of big crowds every night. It was the showpiece of the Southern League at that time."

Showalter was the 1980 opening day DH for the Sounds. In that season, Showalter appeared in 142 games, batting a league-leading .323 (178-for-550) with one home run and 82 RBI's. The 178 hits remains

Buck Showalter played for the Sounds (1980-84) and led the Southern League in batting in 1982 and 1984. *Courtesy of the Nashville Sounds.*

a Southern League record. Showalter also played in leftfield and first base. That 1980 team was managed by Stump Merrill, but lost in the Western Division playoffs to Memphis, three games to one.

"With the team we had, I was lucky to be somewhere in the line-up," said Showalter. "That was a great summer in my life. One of the best things that happened to me in Nashville was I met my wife there. The crowds were so large they had to rope off the outfield to put in the overflow fans."

"I remember the Oak Ridge Boys, Conway Twitty and the National Anthem sung by some of the best I've ever heard. One night it would be Boots Randolph with his saxophone; one night someone would play a harmonica or a fiddle. We all had to scramble out to see who was going to sing. I remember seeing Lorrie Morgan before she was known."

The next season, Showalter would split time with Nashville and Triple-A Columbus. He played in 90 games for the Sounds batting .264 (81-for-307) with no home runs and 38 RBI's. In Columbus, he appeared in 14 games and batted .189. One obstacle for Showalter in settling in at first base was a newcomer to the Sounds in 1981—Don Mattingly.

"Donnie did a lot for my career because I knew rather quickly that I was not going to be the leftfielder or first baseman for the Yankees," said Showalter. "It was fun watching him play. We had some fabulous players like Willie McGee, Steve Balboni, Pat Tabler and some great pitching to come through Nashville. Back then just because you had a great season doesn't mean you are going to advance."

"The Yankees were loaded everywhere. The old joke was the only team that could beat the Yankees was their Triple-A club. I hit .323 in Nashville and was back there the next season. It was just part of the deal. There was not a sense of entitlement. You had to earn it everyday."

In 1982, Showalter was back in Nashville for another full season. Once again he led the Southern League in hits (152) while batting (.294). Johnny Oates was now the Sounds manager in a year that Nashville would end the season in dramatic style. After winning the SL Western Division play-offs, the Sounds would face Jacksonville in the best-of-five championship series.

Nashville led the series two games to one in Greer Stadium and in the bottom of the 13th inning with the game tied 3-3, and two outs Showalter was on base. Brian Dayett, the league-leader in home runs (34), clubbed a home run to win the game (5-3) and the Southern League title.

"Not that I can remember every pitch of it," said Showalter. "But that was an old trivia question. 'Who scored the winning run in that Sounds championship game?' It was me since I was ahead of Dayett. That was a culmination of a lot of stuff. We probably had a better club in 1980, but got beat in the playoffs to Tom Kelly's Orlando Twins club.

"They had all those guys that played on the Twins' World Series championship club. It doesn't happen that much any longer having dominating teams each year since teams don't stay together for a long period of time."

In 1983, Showalter began the season in Nashville batting .276 with one home run and 37 RBI's in 89 games. He finished the season in Columbus hitting .238 in 18 games. Showalter did have some fun in one game with the

Sounds that season when he pitched. His pitching stats that season for the Sounds included one inning, two hits, one earned run and a strikeout for a 9.00 ERA.

"I was one of those guys that wanted to save the pitching staff when games were out of reach," said Showalter. "I did pitch two innings in Columbus later that season and didn't give up a hit or any runs. I threw a lot of batting practice towards the end of my career. I could throw it over the plate so they didn't have to use anybody else. It was just a matter of checking your ego and go out there and take it like a man."

Farrell Owens was the Sounds' general manager (1978-82) and introduced Showalter to a Soundette who would become his wife. They were married on March 5, 1983.

"Angela worked at Opryland and had a few jobs working her way through college," said Showalter. "There are guys that will tell you, 'if you need any help, let me know.' And usually those guys cannot be found when you need them. Farrell was always there. He had a great way about himself.

"He didn't take himself too seriously and you could joke with him. At the end of the day he was a guy you could count on for help traveling around and doing different stuff. Farrell gave great advice about a lot of things that young players were faced with. We were very fortunate to have him around. He was a great buffer for us."

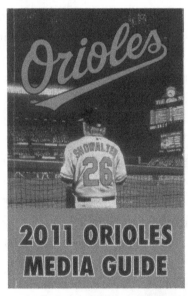

Buck Showalter has been the Baltimore Orioles manager since 2011. *Courtesy of the Baltimore Orioles.*

The 1983 season would be Showalter's last as a player. Though he was just 27 years old, he never made it on a major league roster. His seven-year minor league career stats include 793 games; batting .294 (841-for-2, 865), 17 home runs with 336 RBI's.

"I had one of three decisions to make," said Showalter. "I could continue to play in Triple-A with the Yankees. I could become a free agent and play in Triple-A with somebody else or I could take a job as a hitting coach in Ft. Lauderdale in the Florida State League with the Yankees.

"I had just gotten married. They gave me the opportunity to continue in the organization I had grown to love. I had always looked at myself realistically and knew the Yankees wanted guys that could hit the ball into the seats. I knew there were a lot of things I could never be able to bring them. If I didn't take this opportunity to go down a different path, I probably would regret it. Whatever reputation I had, I wanted to build on in the same organization that knew me. I took them up on it and became a coach."

Showalter would become a minor league manager with Oneonta (1985-86), Ft. Lauderdale (1987-88), and Albany (1989). He would see other duties with the Yankees organization including service as a coach. In 1992, he became the Yankees' manager replacing Stump Merrill his manager in Nashville.

Two years later, Showalter was named American League Manager-of-the-Year after leading the Yankees to a 70-43 record in a season shortened due to a players strike. The strike began on August 12 with the playoffs and World Series eventually cancelled. Showalter managed the Yankees (1992-95), Arizona (1998-200) and Texas (2003-06). He won a second AL Manager-of-the-Year award with Texas (2004).

Showalter has been the Orioles' manager since 2010 and earned his third AL Manager-of-the-Year award in 2014. In that season, Baltimore won the AL Eastern Division. His career managing record through 2016 is 1,429-1,315. Before signing with the Orioles, Showalter worked as an ESPN in-studio analyst.

Showalter would begin wearing jersey No. 11 as a major league manager until switching to No. 26 when he joined the Orioles. Johnny Oates was an Orioles player, coach, and manager that died in 2004. He was also one of Showalter's managers in Nashville (1982).

"Johnny was just a classy man," said Showalter. "He was a guy that was very competitive and understood the human part of baseball and frailties.

Johnny was very driven and played a big role in my life. He showed me by example. I got to know his wife and kids. I thought with their permission it would be a very nice way to honor him while keeping him in everybody's thoughts with the kind of human being and man he was."

Showalter was asked if he was disappointed in never making to the major leagues as a player.

"I don't look at it that way," Showalter said. "I felt like being in Nashville and in other places that I was in the major leagues. It was all a state of mind. It's all relevant rather it is the state high school championship or the Southern League championship. It is in different stages, different coverage so to speak like with the media. All things happen for a reason. I'm lucky and everyday I'm honored to be apart of baseball for another day."

The New York Yankees Visit Greer Stadium

The Yanks are coming! The Yanks are coming!

That was the excitement generated when the 1981 New York Yankees were scheduled to play an exhibition game in Greer Stadium. Baseball's most historic team last played in Nashville in 1953 at the old Sulphur Dell ballpark.

The Yankees were in the second year as the parent club of the hometown Double-A Nashville Sounds, members of the Southern League. Mickey Mantle was one of the stars to have played in 1953 and 28 years later, Reggie Jackson was the Yankee big gun.

The game between the Sounds and Yankees drew an overflowing, standing room only crowd of 17, 318 fans. At this time was the era of George Steinbrenner's revolving managers, and Gene Michael was in Nashville that April 16 afternoon to lead the Bronx Bombers.

The season had already begun when the exhibition game was played. New York was on a day off traveling from Toronto for a game the next night in Texas. Jackson had been nursing a leg injury and was coming off the disabled list. He joined the team in Nashville and was inserted into the lineup as the designated hitter.

Starting for the Stump Merrill's Sounds was pitcher Dan Led Duke, while the Yankees countered with left-hander John Pacella. One other interesting note, Jackson was joining his new teammate Dave Winfield. The future Hall of Famer was in his first season in Yankee pinstripes after playing eight seasons in San Diego while becoming a free agent.

History repeated itself when in 1953 the Yankees swamped the Vols, 9-1. Only 2, 693 fans attended that game. Jackson led the latest version of Yankees to a 10-1 rout of the Sounds. He drove in four runs with a double

New York Yankees owner George Steinbrenner (left) with Sounds owner Larry Schmittou in the Nashville locker room. *Courtesy of Larry Schmittou.*

and single in five plate appearances. Though he didn't hit a home run, the fans were still entertained when Jackson drove a couple of long foul balls out of the park. Batting left-handed, Jackson dropped his bat and glared as the ball quickly left the stadium.

The Yankees collected 12 hits in the victory while Pacella earned the win in five innings of work. Led Duke took the loss after pitching just three innings while giving up seven hits and three runs. Other prominent Yankees to appear in the game were Willie Randolph, Graig Nettles, Bucky Dent, Lou Piniella, Bobby Murcer and future Sounds manager Johnny Oates. Winfield batted once recording a single and a run scored.

Steinbrenner attended the game and said, "The Yankees looked good, but Nashville had to be a little nervous. There is a lot of difference between the major leagues and Class AA ball. But the Sounds got seven hits off Yankee pitching and that isn't bad. I saw four or five youngsters who I'll bet will be on major league rosters within the next couple of years."

Maybe the most popular Yankee that day was Hall of Famer Yogi Berra, a coach. Berra delighted the fans by taking time before and after the game to sign autographs. He also played on that Yankees team in the 1953 exhibition game. Other familiar names on the team, but didn't see action was Goose Gossage, Ron Guidry, Tommy John and Bob Watson.

"I just wish we had played better," Merrill said. "I think the kids were a little nervous. But it was a good experience for us. Most of our guys haven't played against many Double-A teams, much less the New York Yankees."

The 1981 Major League season was a disaster while losing fans. The owners and players could not reach a working agreement. The owners wanted to control skyrocketing salaries with a salary cap. Therefore the players went on strike for 50 days from mid-June until the end of July.

When the strike was resolved, a controversial split-season format was established. The Yankees were given the championship of the "first" season, but fell to sixth in the "second" season. With the poor second half showing, Michael was replaced by Bob Lemon.

New York did beat Milwaukee and Kansas City in the playoff system to earn the American League pennant. However, the Yankees lost to the Dodgers, four games to two in the World Series.

The Sounds made it to the Southern League championship series after beating Memphis in the Western Division finals. Orlando won the SL championship by beating the Sounds, three games to one. Jackson left the Yankees after five seasons to play for the Angels.

New York was back in Nashville in April 1983 without Jackson, but with Winfield the club leader. The roster was noticeably different from two years earlier. Billy Martin was now the Yankees manager with Berra still as popular as ever as a coach. The attendance was 13, 641 on a sunny afternoon. Don Holmquist was the Sounds manager.

New York would take a 4-0 lead over the Sounds going into the bottom of the ninth inning. They pounded out 13 hits off six Nashville pitchers. Doyle Alexander started for the Yankees pitching four innings. Gossage followed him in the fifth inning, Jay Howell in the sixth and seventh innings while Rudy May relieve in the eighth.

Sounds pitcher Mark Shiflett started and pitched three scoreless innings, but gave up two runs in the fourth. The Yankees scored on a single by Ken Griffey, a double by Rick Cerone, a sacrifice fly by Andre Robertson and a single by Barry Evans. Mike Browning relieved Shiflett in the fifth inning and gave up two more runs. Former Sound Don Mattingly and Oscar Gamble each singled, then a sacrifice fly by Roy Smalley followed by two more singles by Griffey and Robertson.

When the Sounds arrived to bat in their half of the ninth, the unexpected happened as Nashville rallied for five runs to defeat the mighty Yankees, 5-4. May gave up a walk and a hit batsman with one out in the ninth. After another out, May again hit a batter and walked in the Sounds first run of the game.

Sounds centerfielder Derwin McNealy's fourth hit of the contest, a two run single to centerfield, cut the

Yogi Berra enjoying the afternoon in the Yankees' dugout in Hershel Greer Stadium in 1983. *Courtesy of Nashville Public Library, Special Collections.*

lead to 4-3. Sounds reserve catcher Frank Kneurer ripped a 2-2 pitch down the left field line to score Matt Gallegos from second and a speedy McNealy from first base for the winning run. Jesus Hernaiz picked up the victory after one inning of relief and May took the loss. Winfield, playing in left, was 1-for-3 in the game.

For security, the Yankees' team charter bus entered the stadium grounds rolling its way around the warning path that led in front on their dugout. Waiting patiently were the Yankees who boarded and left for the Nashville airport for a flight to Arlington, Texas. They finished the season in third place (91-71) seven games behind the Baltimore Orioles.

The Sounds finished 88-58 in second place in the Southern League Western Division. They lost to Birmingham three games to one in the division finals.

Skeeter Barnes: A Sounds' Fan Favorite

This interview between former Sounds' player Skeeter Barnes and Bill Traughber is from 2013.

In the history of the Nashville Sounds, only two players' jersey numbers have been retired. One was Don Mattingly (1981) and the other Skeeter Barnes (1979, 1988-90). Mattingly wore No. 18 while Barnes donned No. 00 in his second stretch with the Sounds.

"I know I did a lot of things there," said Barnes. "One of those years the team was Double-A, but I guess they combined all the numbers whether it was Double-A or Triple-A. I never had my number retired in anything, not even in high school. I didn't wear that number my first year in Nashville. I thought saying nothing to nothing means nothing to nothing so double 00's here we go.

"I was grateful that people appreciated the way I played in Nashville. That's the one thing I've prided myself on. I always played hard wherever I played. Maybe not always good, but I've always played 100 percent and people really supported me."

Barnes was born in Cincinnati, Ohio with the name William Henry Barnes, graduating from Woodward High in 1975 and attended the University of Cincinnati. As for the name "Skeeter" Barnes said, "that's something my mom gave me at birth. It doesn't really mean anything. They just started calling me Skeeter as a newborn and it just kind of stuck."

The Reds selected him in the 16th round of the 1978 major league draft. Barnes was sent to Billings, MT in the Pioneer League for rookies for the remainder of that year. In Billings, he batted .368 in 68 games and was selected to the All-Star Team. He was sent to the Reds Double-A affiliate in Nashville the next season. The Sounds were beginning their second season in Nashville.

"Nashville was a very easy place to play," said Barnes. "A lot of that had to do with Larry Schmittou. I think when it comes to minor league general managers or owners they have to do a good job. Larry was way ahead of his time as far as knowing how to put people into seats. And to make sure there was a competitive team.

Skeeter Barnes played in the major leagues with Cincinnati, Montreal, St. Louis and Detroit finding his most success with the Tigers (1991-94). *Courtesy of the Detroit Tigers.*

"I hear a lot of the kids I work with today talk about how it's hard to play with nobody in the stands. That's always an excuse, but I know in Nashville you had sellout crowds. The outfield was roped off to accommodate more fans. You couldn't wait to get to the ballpark. A lot of that had to do with Larry Schmittou and his family."

The Sounds manager that season was George Scherger, a baseball veteran player with 14 seasons in the Dodgers' minor league system and 10 of those being a player/coach. He managed in the minor leagues from 1947-1967 and then joined the Reds coaching staff in 1970.

"George Scherger was very instrumental in my development," said Barnes. "I owe a lot to the Reds. When I was coming up at the time they didn't skimp on player development. I really learned how to play the game in the Reds system. I have to give the Reds kudos for that. I couldn't say enough about George. The good thing that I liked when I went from rookie ball to Double-A, I was in there with some older players.

"Those first two weeks in that league I was calling home telling my dad they were throwing breaking balls. After awhile I got the hang of it. I settled in. There was so much thrown at you, especially in the first full year where normal guys would probably have played another year of A-ball. George Scherger was on me. He was hard, but he was fair. I had a lot to learn in a short period of time.

"I thank God that I was there because when I look at all the Single-A teams that I cover now, there is a lot of silly immature stuff that goes on. I went from rookie ball to Double-A and I'm thrown in there with guys that had been in Double-A a year or two or maybe in Triple-A. They just didn't go for the shenanigans. I played with a group of guys that when I did something wrong they'd let me know."

With Barnes playing third base and in the outfield, the Sounds were involved with a championship. Nashville defeated Memphis two games to one in the first round of the Western Division playoffs. They would then win the Southern League crown by whipping Columbus, three games to one.

"We won the championship in rookie ball and now I am in my second year in pro ball and win another championship," said Barnes. "We had a slew of guys from that team that made it to the big leagues. It didn't surprise me that we won the championship now that I look back. Guys like Eddie Milner, Paul Householder, Duane Walker, Scotty Brown, Dave van Gorder and Rafael Santo Domingo.

"Gene Menees and Rick Duncan did not make it to the big leagues, but Gene was very instrumental in us winning the championship. To this day, I still can't believe that Gene didn't make it to the big leagues. He was about as fundamentally sound as a second baseman you could ask for. Playing with these guys helped me in my development."

Barnes played in 145 games batting .266 (133-for-500) with 12 home runs, 77 RBI's, 19 doubles and four triples in Nashville. The next year the Yankees became the Sounds next major league affiliate through 1984, followed by Detroit (1985-86).

Barnes made his major league debut in September 1983 with the Reds. In 15 games, he batted .206 (7-for-34). He played mostly for minor league clubs thereafter, but did appear in 19 games for Montreal (1985) and four games in St. Louis (1987). The Reds returned to Nashville as an affiliate in 1987 as a Triple-A team in the American Association. Barnes also returned to Nashville in 1988 as property of Cincinnati.

Was Barnes disappointed about being back in Nashville and another minor league team?

"Wherever I played, I played as hard as I could," said Barnes. "The game is not always fair. It would have been great to get 10 full years in the big leagues, but I didn't. I've never been a guy like that. You have to fall into the right situation like I did in Detroit '91. I always felt I had a chance to go to the big leagues. That is one of the reasons I kept playing."

The Sounds managerial situation was unusual in 1988. Jack Lind began the season as the Sounds skipper, but left the club due to health reasons. Pitching coach Wayne Garland filled in as an interim until Scherger returned as manager. Scherger retired after one game. Jim Hoff replaced Scherger, but departed for a Reds' front office position. Former Texas manager Frank Lucchesi was brought in to finish the season.

Skeeter Barnes wore jersey No. 00 in his second stint with the Sounds that was retired by the team. *Courtesy of the author.*

"Frank kept me on his team when he probably could have said, oh, he is an older guy and we don't need him here," said Barnes. "But he knew that I could play hard and show the younger kids how to play the game. Frank didn't need me on his team. He wanted me on his team.

"Being an older guy I prided in taking care of myself. If you are an older guy and you don't stand out, there is no reason for them to keep you around.

I always felt I could get back to the big leagues and I always stood out when I played."

In his first of three seasons in Nashville (1988), Barnes appeared in 101 games batting .259 (85-for-328) with four home runs and 34 RBI's. The next season, he led the American Association with 39 doubles to earn a spot on the postseason All-Star Team. That season he batted .303 (143-for-472) with six home runs and 55 RBI's.

In his final season in Nashville, Barnes led the American Association with 156 hits (batted .285) and ranked among the leaders with runs scored (83) and collected 34 stolen bases. The Sounds made it to the American Association championship series, losing to Omaha, three games to two.

At age 34, Barnes made it back to the major leagues with Detroit, playing in his most productive years at that level. After batting .330 in 1991 at the Tigers' Triple-A club in Toledo, Barnes was called up to Detroit where he remained until three years later. Barnes played several positions and used primarily as a utility man, which made a valuable asset to the team.

Playing for the Tigers in four seasons, Barnes batted .289, .273, .281 and .286. During all or parts of nine seasons in the major leagues, Barnes played in 353 games, batted .259 (159-for-614), with 14 home runs and 83 RBI's. His minor league career totals include a .296 average (1,773 for 5985) with 121 home runs and 900 RBI's in 1,633 games in 15 seasons.

Barnes ranks as one of the all-time fan favorites at Greer Stadium and currently stands as the Sounds career leader in hits (517), doubles (94), at bats (1,898) and games played (514). He ranks in the top three in every major offensive category on the career leader board. In four seasons as a Sounds player, Barnes batted .280 with 29 home runs and 232 RBI's.

In the early 1990's the Sounds commissioned a miniature statue of Barnes as a fan giveaway at Greer Stadium. Barnes is posed batting left-handed though he actually bats and throws right-handed. A photo of Barnes was used as a model for the statue. It was learned later that the photo was of Barnes kidding around posing as a left-handed batter.

After retiring as a player after the 1994 season, he remained in the game as a minor league coach and manager. Barnes is currently the Minor League

Outfield and Base Running Coordinator for the Tampa Bay Rays. He is in his 11th season in the Tampa Bay organization (seventh in his current position).

Some baseball players are said to be "in between" players. That is a player that is solid in Triple-A, but struggles at the major league level.

"I was a Four-A player," said Barnes. "You are always hoping for that chance in the right position on a big league team. I got there [Detroit] in 1991 and fit right in, playing the same way for the last five years. And they'd ask where had you been the before here. I'd say I've been in Nashville. It's just the matter of finding the right fit."

The Nashville Xpress

During the 1993 and 1994 seasons, Herschel Greer Stadium became the home for two baseball franchises. When the Charlotte Knights moved up from Double-A in the Southern League to the Triple-A International League prior to the 1993 season, it left a vacancy in the league.

Triple-A (American Association) Nashville Sounds president Larry Schmittou offered Greer Stadium as a temporary solution. The Nashville Xpress came into existence. The Xpress would schedule home games during the Sounds road trips. Nashville fans would be able to see baseball nearly every day.

It marked the first time in 21 years that two minor league teams shared a city. *Baseball America* presented its assessment of the two-team experiment when in its "Top 10 happenings in minor league baseball" the Nashville pair of teams topped the list.

"I regard it as the perfect summer," said Schmittou in an interview with the *Tennessean*. "Actually, by having two teams we have eased some of our problems in terms of seasonal help. We can schedule off-days and provide full-time employment over the summer for a number of people.

"We'll be under a microscope a little bit, but that has more pluses than minuses. We are going to attract a lot of attention—things like the *Baseball America* mention. If we do well, and I hope we do, it can only be a feather in our cap."

The new Nashville Xpress went 40-31 to take the first half Western Division title, but the Minnesota Twins' farm team fell to 32-39 in the second half and were swept in best-of-five playoffs by the eventual league champion

The Double-A Nashville Xpress shared Herschel Greer Stadium with the Triple-A Sounds for two seasons. *Courtesy of Jeremy Jones.*

Birmingham Barons. Phil Roof managed the Xpress. The Xpress drew 179,000 fans that season.

Rich Becker was the team's only All-Star, batting .287, stealing 29-of-36 base attempts, drawing 94 walks and scoring 93 runs. The team was led in home runs by Marty Cordova with 19, but Cordova also struck out a league-leading 153. Oscar Munoz did not make the All-Star team, but was named the Most Valuable Pitcher with an 11-4 record and a 3.08 ERA. He struck out 136 batters in 139 innings. Other members of the Express starting rotation include: Brad Radke (2-6, 4.62), Todd Ritchie (3-2, 3.66) and Eddie Guardado (4-0, 1.24).

In 1994, the team went 74-66 under Roof, but did not claim a crown in either half. They drew 135,048 fans. The Xpress led the Southern League with a 3.40 ERA and had two of the top six prospects in the circuit—LaTroy Hawkins (#2 prospect, 9-2, 2.33) and Marc Barcelo (#6 prospect, 11-6, 2.65).

The pitching staff also featured Rich Garces (4-5, 3.72), Radke (12-9, 2.66), and Erik Schullstrom (1-2, 2.63 and eight saves). Catcher Damian Miller hit .268 and went on to a career best of all 1994 Xpress position players The offensive star was second baseman Mitch Simons who hit .317 to tie for second in the SL batting for average. Simons also stole 30-of-39 base attempts.

Also in 1994 Michael Jordan, who was in his first retirement from the NBA Chicago Bulls, played in the outfield for the Birmingham Barons, a rival of the Xpress. If Jordan had been promoted to Triple-A, he would have played for the Sounds, the White Sox top farm club.

The next season, the temporary housing situation was resolved when the Xpress moved to Wilmington, N.C. and became the Port City Roosters.

Michael Jordan Plays Baseball in Nashville

Michael Jordan was arguably the greatest basketball player on the planet Earth. After winning his third consecutive NBA championship with the Chicago Bulls in 1993, Jordan announced his retirement. His father had been murdered in July of that year and he lost his desire to play the game. Jordan did not leave sports for long. In the following spring, Jordan surprised the sports world when he signed a minor league baseball contract with the Double-A Birmingham Barons of the Southern League.

At this time, Nashville baseball was in a unique situation. The Double-A Nashville Express of the Southern League shared Greer Stadium with the Triple-A Nashville Sounds. When one team was on the road, the other was in Nashville. This would give Nashvillians a chance to see Jordan play baseball.

A Birmingham newspaper wrote about life in the minor leagues for one of the world's richest sports figures:

"He rents a $450,000 home on the area's most prestigious golf course. He parks his black Porsche in a private, fenced-in area at Hoover Metropolitan Stadium, and has a police escort to the freeway most nights.

"Rather than scrunch his long legs in a regular bus seat and strain his neck to see one of three TV monitors, Michael Jordan shelled out $330,000 to buy the Birmingham Barons a new bus that had extra leg room, six TV's and a lounge.

"Jordan insists that he is just another Double-A ballplayer chasing a boyhood dream, but the only things the retired basketball star seems to have in common with his roommates is his salary—reportedly $850 a month—and the $16 meal allowance he gets on road trips.

NBA legend Michael Jordan played baseball in seven games in Herschel Greer Stadium (1994) where he was 4-for-32 at the plate. *Courtesy of the Birmingham Barons.*

"Nobody else on the Barons roster has autograph-hungry fans at the stadium four hours before game time. Nobody else has replicas of his jersey on sale at the nearby Riverchase Galleria Mall. Nobody else had 130 reporters at his locker opening night, including two from Germany and Japan."

In April 1994, that Jordan circus arrived in Nashville for a two-game series. After his first nine games, Jordan was hitting .333 with one RBI and four stolen bases. In his first appearance at Greer before 16,842 fans, the right-fielder was 1-for-4 with an RBI single. Jordan made an impression immediately in the first inning, which Jimmy Davy of the *Tennessean* wrote:

"Michael Jordan did a 360 last night at Greer Stadium and it wasn't a dunk. It was a first-inning, head-spinning catch of a fly ball near the right field fence, during which Jordan whirled two or three directions and made the catch tumbling to the turf.

"The celebrated outfielder for the Birmingham Barons of the Class AA Southern League held up the ball. And the crowd went wild. Jordan then loped in from the outfield to a standing ovation, the first of many he would get from the partisan throng."

In his first at-bat, Jordan grounded out on a play from third to first that wasn't close. But the fans booed the first base umpire anyway. In the fourth inning, Jordan slammed a single off the glove of the Xpress pitcher that drove in a run to give the Barons a 2-1 lead. The fans really went crazy when Jordan stole second base.

The next night another 16,000-plus fans witnessed Jordan going 1-for-4 with a stolen base in the Xpress 5-3 victory. When Jordan was standing in his right field position, fans tried to overload that side of the stadium for a closer look or a better camera shot. When he moved to third base after a teammate walked, that side of the stadium became unbalanced. Wherever MJ went, the fans wanted to be.

When Jordan, wearing jersey No. 45, came back to Nashville a month later, he was not such a hot item as far as drawing fans or at the plate. Jordan's second trip into Greer for a three-game series came with a .209 batting average and a slump. In his first game, Jordan was 0-for-4 while reaching base on an error. Just 5,083 fans were in attendance.

In the second game, before 10,206 fans, Jordan was 1-for-3 with a single. He was in the midst of a 1-for-20 skid. Said Xpress winning pitcher LaTroy Hawkins after the game on facing Jordan, "It was a big thrill. I'm definitely

After deciding he wasn't progressing enough, the Barons' outfielder quit minor league baseball after one season and returned to the NBA.

waking my folks up to tell them about this. He hit a fastball. The man is so damn cool, though. I've kind of been talking to him for a while."

Jordan was 0-for-3 in the third game. Over 11,000 fans watched Jordan's batting average dip to .203. In the ninth inning, Jordan was given the bunt sign with no outs and a teammate on first base. Jordan laid down a perfect bunt to advance the runner. Two runs would score that inning to give the Barons the eventual victory.

Jordan made his final appearances in Nashville in June and August. In a June doubleheader, Jordan was 0-for-6 in a Barons sweep, but sat out the next day's final game of the series. Two months later, Jordan went 1-for-8 in a doubleheader, but scored the winning run in the nightcap. The Sounds and Barons split the doubleheader before 7,290 fans.

For that season, Jordan appeared in 127 games, batted .202 (88-for-436); scored 46 runs, recorded 116 total bases (17 doubles, 1 triple, 3 home runs); 51 RBI's; 51 walks; 30 stolen bases and committed 11 errors. Jordan retired from baseball and went back to playing for the Bulls and the NBA where he won three more consecutive championships.

In 13 NBA seasons, Jordan won the MVP award five times; six Finals MVPs; Rookie of the Year (1985); 10 time All-NBA First Team; 12 time All-Star and Defensive Player of the Year (1998). Jordan was enshrined into the Naismith Memorial Basketball Hall of Fame in 2009.

"My first season playing baseball was filled with both highs and lows, with the lows taking place more often than not," Jordan once said about his lone baseball season. "It was when these lows took over that that I'd sit back and think about whether or not I had gotten myself too far in over my head with this game.

"At one point my game got so shaky it kind of reinforced some previous doubts. But continuing to play at such a poor level really made me question playing at all. I needed to know if I wasting my time or not.

"I approached my manager Terry Francona and explained to him that I had developed some reservations about my level of performance. If he had said, 'You're wasting your time, Mike.' I would have walked away from the game then and there, but instead he reassured me I was not."

When Jordan and Francona were looking for the new bus for the Barons, the first one the 31-year old rookie chose was too small. Said Francona to Jordan, "Michael, that one is really nice—for you and me."

Oak Ridge Boys' Richard Sterban:
Official Ambassador of the Sounds

This exclusive interview between Richard Sterban of the Oak Ridge Boys and Bill Traughber is from 2014. In that year, Sterban was given his own bobblehead night and tossed the ceremonial first pitch in Greer Stadium. Sterban once sang backup with Elvis Presley (while with the Stamps Quartet) before joining the Oak Ridge Boys in 1972.

If there were a nominating process for the biggest baseball fan in Nashville, Richard Sterban of the Oak Ridge Boys would receive a lot of votes. His passion for baseball goes back to his early youth as a small child.

"When I first moved to Nashville, the only baseball that I could find was going out to Vanderbilt," said Sterban who was born in Camden, New Jersey. "That's how I first met Larry Schmittou. He was the Vandy coach at the time. I loved baseball so much I just had to get my baseball fix so I'd go to Vandy games. When I read in the paper that he [Schmittou] was going to bring baseball back to Nashville, I thought I would drive over and talk to him. I wanted to see how I could get involved. He was an owner and general manager and they were in the process of building the stadium.

"Schmittou had a little shack for an office that was near where rightfielder is today. I explained to him that I was an avid baseball fan and I wanted to get involved with this new venture of his. That first season, I came to all the games and he let me hang out. I got to know Chuck Goggin our first manager that year. After the first season he called me and said he figured out a way for me to get involved. I purchased a small percentage pf the team from one of the other owners. I was one of the owners of the Nashville Sounds."

Richard Sterban receives the baseball from Sounds' pitcher Arcenio Leon after throwing out the ceremonial first pitch in Herschel Greer Stadium. *Courtesy of the Nashville Sounds.*

The first Sounds general manager was Farrell Owens. He once saw the Oak Ridge Boys each wearing Sounds jackets during an interview on a national television program after the first year. Owens said that type of publicity for the new Double-A baseball club was priceless.

"I personally have worn my Sounds jersey on television shows, stadiums and numerous occasions like at 'Fan Fair,' Sterban said. "Right now I am wearing my Vanderbilt baseball jersey that Maggie, Tim Corbin's wife, got for me. And I'm wearing my Vandy baseball cap. I am really into it big time. I got so much pleasure watching Prince Fielder win the Home Run Derby [2014 MLB All-Star game] since he is a former Nashville Sound and Sandy Guerrero [Sounds hitting coach] pitching to him.

"That was the coolest thing. I watched on television Ryan Braun being interviewed and he mentioned playing with R.A. Dickey when he was with the Sounds. That was great for the Sounds. That night I texted Sandy and told him he did a great job of pitching. He texted me back to let me know that he would be in Nashville so we could hang out around the batting cage."

As an owner of the Sounds, Sterban would travel with the team on the road especially at training camps.

"I did travel quite often during the Double-A days," said Sterban. "I actually took some of those bus rides with the guys on road trips. I will still fly sometimes when they are on the road. I've often flown to playoff games like a few years ago to Sacramento to watch them play."

Being as close to the team as he was, Sterban would meet some of the biggest names associated with major league baseball. With the several parent clubs connected with the Sounds, Sterban would have the privilege of expanding his baseball experiences. Some of the top greats in baseball that ventured through Nashville were related to the New York Yankees [1980-84].

"I've got a great picture on the wall in my den of me, Mickey Mantle, and Whitey Ford in the Sounds clubhouse before any renovations had been done to Greer," Sterban said. "This was back when we were associated with the Yankees. Larry Schmittou had some type of promotion he arranged involving Ford and Mantle. He called me to ask if I wanted to meet with those guys to come down early. So I went down there in the middle of the afternoon and had a photo taken with both of them. That photo is one of my prized possessions."

The thing Sterban enjoys the most is being around baseball players. He has met more baseball men who have become friends. Some of these ballplayers were with the Sounds and went on to contribute to the National Pastime's history.

"Back in the Double-A days I got to know Buck Showalter who is now the manager of the Baltimore Orioles," Sterban said. "I got to know Don Mattingly when he was here for one year. Over the years I've been able to hang out with players, including the Milwaukee Brewers.

The Oak Ridge Boys prepare to sing the National Anthem before a Sounds game. Left to right: Richard Sterban, William Lee Golden, Duane Allen and Joe Bonsall. *Courtesy of the Nashville Sounds.*

"I remember a day where there was a rain delay and the game was eventually postponed. The players were sitting in the Sounds clubhouse just waiting and they allowed me to join them. I sat there telling them stories about Johnny Cash and country music stories. Prince Fielder was sitting right there with me during that rain delay. It was a cool thing."

Sterban said that the two most memorable home runs he witnessed at Greer Stadium were by Erik Peterson and Steve Balboni. Both dingers were hit well over the centerfield wall. A highlight for Sterban was in 1979 when the Sounds clinched their first playoff berth for the playoffs. Sterban joined the team on the field and in the old clubhouse to celebrate.

Not only did Sterban mingle with Nashville Sounds players off the field, he also joined them on the field as a teammate.

"I actually got into a Nashville Sounds box score," said Sterban. "In 1986, the Nashville Sounds went to Huntsville to play in a exhibition game against the Stars. As a promotional gimmick, they had me suit up and coach first base. I was a part owner of the Huntsville Stars and Sounds; they were tied together. It was a thrilling experience for me. We got towards the end of the game when Scotti Madison asked me if I was ready to go in. He told me they wanted to put me in the for the last inning in right field. I said I couldn't do that.

"The Sounds manager at the time was Leon Roberts and he said we are going to put you in right field in the last inning when there are two outs. That way you can get your name in the box score. So Scotti Madison told me to go down to the bullpen with him to throw the ball and warm up. I was already in a Sounds uniform. So I went down there, warmed up with Scotti Madison and sure enough when there were two outs in the ninth inning they announced my name and put me in right field.

"I don't remember who the centerfielder was, but he came over to me and said, 'don't worry, I've got you covered.' And I was praying that the ball wasn't hit to me. The last out was a ground ball in the infield. The team was laughing at me the entire time because I was standing too close to the foul line. I was almost afraid to get too far onto the field. The next day in the newspaper they had 'Sterban' in the box score. That box score is one of my most prized possessions."

Maybe the most pleasant experience Sterban has received with the Sounds was when the new ownership came to Nashville in 2008, and declared him the official Ambassador of the Nashville Sounds.

"There is no question that it is an honor for me to be named the official Sounds ambassador," said Sterban. "I am no longer a Sounds owner, but for 30 years I was an owner. I've gotten to know Frank Ward who came in a few years ago and bought all of us out. They have allowed me to be involved with the team and I do appearance that.

"The Nashville Sounds have been a passion of mine for decades. It has been my little toy that I play with on the side. Even though I am no longer an owner, I still walk into Greer Stadium and feel like I am an owner. They make me feel like I am very much part of the team."

First Tennessee Park

Serious talks about replacing aging Herschel Greer Stadium began in 2008 with plans for a much needed new downtown ballpark. However, that project, known as First Tennessee Field, was eventually abandoned. Updates and repairs to Greer were necessary to help meet the Triple-A standards until the fate of a new ballpark became a reality.

In 2013, Nashville Mayor Karl Dean and other city officials drafted plans that included public and private financing at a cost of $75 million for the land acquisition and construction of the new state-of-the-art ballpark. A 1,000-car parking garage was included in the plans.   •

The site chosen was on a portion of the old Sulphur Dell ballpark once home to the Nashville Vols (1901-62, 1963). Since the old ballpark was demolished in 1969 that site was used mostly as a state-operated surface parking lots located near the Bicentennial Mall. Baseball had been played on that location since the 1860's.

"Sulphur Dell sat between Fourth and Fifth Avenues," said Farrell Owens who played youth baseball in Sulphur Dell. "Jackson Street (now renamed Jim Gilliam Way) ran beyond the left field fence toward center field between Fourth and Fifth. The old Fourth Avenue would now run from home plate through second base on out to center field of the new ballpark. Home plate in Sulphur Dell would now be in the right field corner of First Tennessee Park."

The city of Nashville owns First Tennessee Park and is leased to the team for 30 years until 2045. A mixed-use plan by the Sounds ownership group implemented a retail development plan for $50 million. Beautiful field and club level suites give each fan a terrific view. Future plans for the area include restaurants, apartments and parking ramps.

The ribbon cutting ceremony before the first game at First Tennessee Park in 2015. Left to right: Cathy Bender, Erica Gilmore, Sounds co-owner Frank Ward, Nashville Mayor Karl Dean (with scissors), Tennessee Governor Bill Haslam, Carol Yochem, Sounds co-owner Masahiro Honzawa and Branch Rickey III. *Courtesy of Mike Strasinger/Nashville Sounds.*

Memphis-based First Tennessee Bank purchased the naming rights to the ballpark for 10 years with a 10-year option. The ballpark's final approval from the Metro Council, State Building Commission and Nashville Sports Authority arrived on December 10, 2013.

The architect for the project was Hastings Architecture Associates, LLC while the project manager was Gobbell Hays Partners, Inc and Capital Project Solutions, Inc. The general contractor was a joint venture of Barton Malow/Bell and Harmony. The structural engineer was Walter P. Moore.

A groundbreaking ceremony took place on January 27, 2014. Attending that event were Mayor Dean, Sounds owner Fred Ward and Minor League Baseball President Pat O'Conner. Hundreds of excited Nashville baseball fans also attended the ceremony.

Excavation on the site began on March 3 where workers soon uncovered artifacts dated to around 1150 AD. Pieces of ceramics and other historic articles were discovered while archaeologists determined the site to be a Native American settlement. In the 1800's, the area was a city cemetery and with the growth of Nashville, the interred were relocated to another portion of the city.

In August, the ballpark began to take shape with the raising of the steel frame and the pouring of concrete. In January 2015, the installation of the 8,500 seats began. A newly designed guitar-shaped scoreboard began its installation on February 23. The next month ground crews began laying the sod while home plate from Greer was transported to the new ballpark.

The first game in First Tennessee Park was scheduled for April 17, with the Colorado Springs Sky Sox. On March 23, tickets for the home opener were placed on sale and sold out in approximately 15 minutes. Including the outfield berm and several standing room areas throughout the ballpark, seating capacity for First Tennessee Park is 10,000. The first game drew a standing-room only crowd of 10,459.

Before the gates were opened allowing fans inside, a ribbon-cutting ceremony was held in front of the ballpark's façade at 4:30 p.m. At the ribbon-cutting were Mayor Dean, team owners Masashiro Honzawa and Fred Ward, Branch Rickey III, President of the Pacific Coast League, Sounds COO Gary Arthur, Oakland A's president Michael Crowley, members of the Metro Council that supported the project and hundreds of fans.

Mayor Dean, wearing a No. 15 Sounds jersey, tossed the ceremonial first pitch. Charles Esten, a star for the ABC television series *Nashville*, performed The Star Spangled Banner. Esten also sang at the ribbon-cutting ceremony. The first promotional giveaway to the first 4,000 fans entering the ballpark was pink piggy banks, sponsored by First Tennessee Bank.

Hanging over the concourse, which circles the playing field, are photos and information on key baseball players that were part of Nashville baseball history. In attendance were former Nashville Vols' players Larry Taylor, Bobby Durnbaugh, Roy Pardue and Buddy Gilbert. After the game, a large fireworks display lit the city skyline.

The Nashville Sounds, managed by Steve Scarsone, line-up for the first game at First Tennessee Park on April 17, 2015 was:

Sounds pitcher Arnold Leon delivers the first pitch in First Tennessee Park's inaugural game. *Courtesy of Mike Strasinger/Nashville Sounds.*

Billy Burns, center field; Joey Wendle, second base; Max Muncy, first base; Bryan Anderson, catcher; Kent Matthes, right field; Jason Pridie, left field; Alden Carrithers, designated hitter; Andy Parrino, shortstop, Niuman Romero, third base and Arnold Leon pitcher.

The Sounds defeated the Colorado Springs Sky Sox 3-2 in 10 innings. Appearing in relief for the Sounds were Pat Venditte, Chad Smith and Ryan Cook. Leon recorded the first strikeout at the park retiring Colorado Springs' leadoff batter Matt Long in the first inning.

Matt Clark of the Sky Sox registered the first hit in the park a single to leftfielder in the second inning. Clark also secured the first RBI for his team in the fourth inning. Nashville's Wendle clubbed the park's first home run four games later on April 21 against Oklahoma City. The Sounds media relations department summed up that first game:

"Baseball came home to Nashville on Friday night and what a homecoming it was. Sounds first baseman Max Muncy hit an RBI double in the tenth inning and the Sounds walked-off over the Colorado Springs Sky Sox at First Tennessee Park. Feeding off the energy from a capacity crowd of 10,459,

Arnold Leon struck out seven batters in four innings. Switch-hitter Pat Venditte succeeded Leon, throwing three scoreless innings. The Nebraska native has thrown 7.2 scoreless innings to start the season.

"Former Sound Matt Clark recorded the first hit in First Tennessee Park history in the second inning. He then provided the first RBI in the fourth inning on a line drive to center field. Ben Guez added another single in the inning and the Sounds trailed 2-0. The Sounds spent no time getting back in it. Joey Wendle and Muncy walked to start the fourth inning and advanced a base each on a Bryan Anderson fly out. Jason Pridie then drove both in on a two-out RBI single.

"Both teams fell silent offensively until Muncy's magical moment in the tenth. Billy Burns led off the inning with a single. The hit gave the speedy outfielder his fourth straight multi-hit game. After Wendle went down swinging, Muncy stepped to the plate. He took the first pitch he saw and hit it off the wall in right. Burns scored easily and the Sounds sprinted from their dugout to celebrate their first home victory.

"Ryan Cook improved to 2-0, while David Goforth suffered his first loss."

The Nashville Sounds posted a 66-78 record in 2015, finishing the campaign third in the American Southern Division in the Pacific Coast League. They were 12 games behind division winner Round Rock for 12th best in the

An aerial view of First Tennessee Park (Courtesy of the Nashville Sounds).

16-team league. Nashville drew 565,548 fans, the fourth best total in the PCL and the most in the franchise's history.

The new ballpark averaged 7,965 fans per game with a season high of 11,482 on June 5 against Salt Lake City. The Sounds were on national television for the first time in franchise history as they welcomed the CBS Sports Network in a sold out game with Salt Lake on June 4.

Outfielder Pridie was named the team's MVP while leading in batting (.310), RBI's (89), home runs (20) and runs scored (84). Wendle was the other stats leader in games played (137), at-bats (577), hits (167), triples (8) and doubles (42). Pitching leaders were Barry Zito ERA (3.46), innings pitched (138) and wins (8). Brad Mills and Ryan Cook tied for the most saves (8). Mills was also the strikeout leader (95) and started the most games (24).

The center field wall is 403 feet from home plate, 330 feet to left field and 310 feet to right field. The past is remembered on the opposite side of the green center field wall in tin lettering "SITE OF SULPHUR DELL, BASEBALL'S MOST HISTORIC BALL PARK 1870-1963." These words were on the facade of the Sulphur Dell ballpark.

Nashville Sounds' Historical Timeline

1978: Larry Schmittou, president, majority owner of the Nashville Sounds and head baseball coach of Vanderbilt University forms an investment group to bring professional baseball to Nashville. A lease is secured with the Nashville Metro Government to build Herschel Greer Stadium on a site located south of downtown Nashville at the foot of St. Cloud Hill in Fort Negley Park.

1978: The Sounds enter into an agreement with the Cincinnati Reds for Nashville to become their Double-A affiliate in the Southern League.

1978: The Nashville Sounds play their first game, on April 15,1978, losing at Memphis, 4-2. Chuck Goggin becomes the Sounds first manager.

Professional baseball would return to Nashville for the first time since 1963 with Herschel Geer Stadium the home of the Sounds. *Courtesy of the Nashville Sounds.*

1978: The next night the Sounds record their first franchise victory with a 3-0 shutout of the Memphis Chicks.

1978: Nashville defeats Savannah, 12-4 in the home opener at Greer Stadium on April, 26. A sellout crowd of 8,156 greets the home team.

1979: On April, 24, Dave van Gorder clubs the Sounds' first grand slam in a game against Jacksonville.

1979: Under Sounds manager George Scherger, the 1979 club defeats Columbus three games to one (best-of-five) to capture the Southern League championship.

1980: The Sounds become affiliates of the New York Yankees. Carl "Stump" Merrill managed Nashville for two seasons. Steve Balboni leads the league in runs (101), home runs (34), RBIs (122) and total bases (288) and is Southern League's MVP. Buck Showalter leads the team in average (.323) and the Southern League in hits (178).

1980: On June 6, Mark Johnston hits the Sounds' first-ever pinch-hit home run, against Chattanooga.

1981: Don Mattingly leads the Sounds in hits (173), RBIs (98) and doubles (35). Nashville is led in average by Willie McGee (.322). Mattingly would win the American League MVP award in 1985 while the National League MVP went to McGee in the same year.

1982: For the second time, Buck Showalter leads the Southern League in hits, with 152.

1982: Pitching for the Sounds, Clay Christiansen and Stefan Wever lead the Southern League in victories (16).

1982: Manager Johnny Oates leads the Sounds to their second championship, defeating Jacksonville three-games-to-one.

1982: The Sounds record their largest crowd ever, on August 18th against Columbus, with 22,315 on hand.

1983: The smallest crowd ever to attend a Sounds game occurs on April 18, with 419 fans braving 36-degree weather.

1984: On May 4, Jim Deshaies tosses the Sounds first no-hitter (7 innings) as Nashville defeats Columbus in the second game of a doubleheader.

Displaying the Sounds first title flag in 1979 are Sounds general manager Farrell Owens (left) and team president Larry Schmittou. *Courtesy of Farrell Owens.*

1985: Nashville becomes the Triple-A affiliate of the Detroit Tigers and joins the American Association.

1985: Bryan Kelly completes a 6-0 no-hitter in Greer Stadium for Nashville in the victory over Oklahoma City on July 17.

1985: Scotti Madison leads the American Association with a .341 batting average.

1986: Bruce Fields of Nashville bats .368 to lead the American Association.

1986: Pitcher John Pacella records the most saves in the American Association with 17.

1987: Nashville enters into its second agreement with the Reds, remaining in the American Association.

1987: Third baseman Chris Sabo plays for the Sounds in 1987 and is later promoted to Cincinnati. He becomes the National League's Rookie-of-the-Year in 1988, a first for any former Sounds player.

1988: During a two-week period, Nashville goes through five managers. Jack Lind leaves due to health issues. Pitching coach Wayne Garland is interim manager until George Scherger is hired. Scherger retires after one game and is replaced by Jim Hoff. Hoff is soon promoted to the Reds front office. Frank Lucchesi finishes out the season.

1988: In Nashville, Jack Armstrong pitches the Sounds' third no-hitter, on August 7, against Indianapolis, 4-0. The night before, Indianapolis hurlers Randy Johnson (7 innings) and Pat Pacillo (1 inning) combined to no-hit the Sounds, but lost the game, 1-0. These are the only back-to-back no-hitters at Greer Stadium.

1988: Sounds Van Snider leads the American Association with 23 home runs.

Nashville first baseman Don Mattingly was the American League's MVP (1985) while playing for the Yankees batting .324 with 35 home runs and 145 RBIs. *Courtesy of the Nashville Sounds.*

1989: Jack Armstrong ties for the American Association league lead in wins with 12.

1990: Skeeter Barnes leads the American Association with 156 hits.

1990: Chris Hammond leads the American Association with 15 victories, a 2.17 ERA and 149 K's. For that effort he is named the American Association's Pitcher-of-the-Year.

1992: Keith Brown and Tim Pugh tie with three other pitchers for most wins (12) in the American Association.

1992: The Sounds set their all-time attendance record in 1992 with 605,122 fans clicking the turnstiles at Greer Stadium.

1993: The iconic guitar-shaped scoreboard is installed at Greer Stadium prior to the season. It is manufactured by Fairtron Corporation and installed by Joslin Sign Company.

1993: Nashville becomes the top affiliate for the Chicago White Sox, remaining in the American Association, and manager Rick Renick is named Manager-of-the-Year.

1993: Sounds Matt Merullo leads the American Association with a .332 batting average.

1994: Pitcher Scott Ruffcorn leads the American Association in victories with 15 and is named the American Association's Pitcher-of-the-Year.

1996: For the second time, Scott Ruffcorn leads the American Association in wins (13).

1996: At the end of the season, Larry Schmittou sells his entire financial interest in the Sounds to Al Gordon, president of AmeriSports Companies, LLC. Schmittou feared that the new NFL team in Nashville (Oilers/Titans) would harm minor league baseball in the city.

1996: Manager Rick Renick is named the American Association's Manager-of-the-Year for the second time.

1997: Sounds outfielder Magglio Ordonez wins every American Association Award for which he was eligible. He became the Most Valuable player, Rookie-of-the-Year and Star-of-Stars (All-Star game MVP).

1998: The Pittsburgh Pirates begin their Triple-A affiliation with the Sounds. The American Association folds and is absorbed into the International League and Pacific Coast Leagues. Nashville joins the Pacific Coast League.

1999: The Sounds enjoy the longest winning streak of their history. From June 2 to June 20, 15 consecutive victories are collected.

2001: Marty Brown becomes the Sounds' 25th manager. He is the first former Nashville Sounds player (1988-89) to serve as the team's skipper.

2001: On June 30 at Tucson, Tike Redman becomes the first Sounds to hit for the cycle: single in the fourth inning, homer in the sixth, double in the seventh and triple in the ninth. The Sounds lose 6-5.

2003: Sounds pitcher John Wasdin tosses a perfect game on April 7, in Nashville. The gem is completed with just 100 pitches in a 4-0 victory over Albuquerque. It was only the second perfect game thrown in the 100-plus year history of the PCL.

2003: Mark Corey is in a two-way tie for the PCL lead with 30 saves.

2004: On May 21, J.R. House becomes the second Sound to hit for the cycle: doubling in the first inning, singling in the third, homering in the fifth and a tripling in the seventh. The game is played in Sacramento in an 8-7 Sounds win.

The iconic Nashville Sounds guitar-shaped scoreboard was constructed in Herschel Greer Stadium (1993). *Courtesy of the Nashville Sounds.*

2005: Remaining in the PCL, Nashville is now affiliated with the Milwaukee Brewers.

2005: Nashville wins the Pacific Coast League title under manager Frank Kremblas. It is the Sounds' third and last championship. Nashville sweeps Tacoma in three games to take the crown.

2006: On May 5-6, the Sounds lose a 24-inning contest to New Orleans 5-4 in Greer Stadium. The official time of the game is eight hours and seven minutes. The game ties for the longest in innings in the 100-plus year history of the PCL.

2006: On July 15, three Sounds pitchers combine for a 2-0 no-hitter in Nashville. The victory over Memphis includes pitchers Carlos Villanueva, Mike Meyers and Alec Zumwalt.

2007: Nashville hurler Manny Parra throws a perfect game on June 25, in Round Rock, Texas. Parra registers 107 pitches while recording 11 strikeouts in the 3-0 victory.

2007: R.A. Dickey leads all Pacific Coast League pitchers with 13 victories and is named the Pacific Coast League's Pitcher-of-the-Year.

2007: Ryan Braun begins the season in Nashville and is later promoted to Milwaukee. The next year Braun becomes the third former Sound to be honored as National League Rookie-of-the-Year.

2007: Sounds manager Frank Kremblas in named the Pacific Coast League's Manager-of-the-Year.

2008: On June 14, the Sounds are in Iowa for a game. Excessive flooding causes a mandatory evacuation of downtown Des Moines. Special permission to play the game is granted, as long as no fans are inside the ballpark. The game is broadcast on radio. The Sounds lose to the Cubs, 5-4.

2008: On October 30, AmeriSports sells their Sounds ownership to MFP Baseball, a New York-based group of investors consisting of Masahiro Honzawa, Steve Posner and Frank Ward.

2010: Chris Smith leads the Pacific Coast League in saves with 26.

2011: On July 10, Caleb Gindl becomes the Sounds third player to hit for the cycle, in a Nashville 9-5 victory in Albuquerque. He triples in the

Sounds pitcher John Wasdin tossed a perfect game for the Sounds at Herschel Greer Stadium on April 7, 2003 striking out 15 batters on 100 pitches. *Courtesy of Mike Strasinger/Nashville Sounds.*

second inning, homers in the third, doubles in the eighth and singles in the ninth.

2011: The Sounds record a triple play on August 20 at Omaha when outfielder Logan Schafer catches a fly ball for the first out. The two base runners on first and second base were off on a hit and run. Schafer fires the ball to second baseman Eric Farris, who touches second base for the second out, and then hurries the ball to first baseman Mat Gamel who steps on first base for the third out.

2013: Right-hander Johnny Hellweg is named the PCL's Pitcher-of-the-Year for 2013. In 23 starts, he records a 12-5 record with a 3.15 ERA.

Nashville Sounds' Record Holders and Milestones

*Skeeter Barnes (1979, 88-90) has played in more Sounds career games (514), recorded the most career hits (517), most career doubles (94) and most plate appearances (1,848).

*Chad Hermansen (1998-2002) scored more career runs (303), most career home runs (92) and most career RBIs (286).

*Otis Nixon (1981-82) collected the Sounds most career-stolen bases with 133.

*Tike Redman (2000-03, 09) has secured the most career triples in Sounds history (32).

*Steve Balboni (1980) and Brian Dayett (1982) are tied with the most home runs in a single season with 34.

*Steve Balboni (1980) also holds the mark for most single-season RBIs (122).

*Bruce Fields (1986) holds the Sounds single season best for highest batting average (.368).

*Gene Menees (1979) and Skeeter Barnes (1979) are tied for playing in the most games in a single season (145).

*Norberto Martin (1993) holds the Sounds single season record for most hits (179).

*Otis Nixon (1981) stole the most bases (72) in one season wearing a Sounds' uniform.

* Tim Dillard (2007-13) has the most career pitching wins with 39 for the Sounds.

*Joey Vierra (1990-92, 94-95) pitched in 238 games, the most in a Sounds career.

Tim Dillard (2007-14) is the Sounds' all-time winningest pitcher with 39 victories (24 losses). *Courtesy of Mike Strasinger/Nashville Sounds.*

*Reliever Mark Corey (2003-04) registered 46 career saves to lead all former Sounds pitchers.

*Jamie Werly (1980-81, 83) totaled 352 strikeouts, most in a Nashville career.

*Clay Christiansen (1982) and Stefan Wever (1982) are tied for the most victories (16) in a season playing for the Sounds.

*Chris Hammond (1980) recorded the lowest ERA (2.17) of any Sounds pitcher in a single year.

*Geoff Combe (1978) appeared in more games (66) as a pitcher for a single season.

*Jamie Werly (1981) struck out 193 batters the most in a single year.

*The Sounds appeared in the playoffs in 1979, 1980, 1981, 1982, 1983, 1984, 1990, 1993,1994, 2003, 2005, 2006, 2007 and 2016.

*There have been two men connected to the Nashville Sounds inducted into the National Baseball Hall of Fame. Hoyt Wilhelm was the Sounds pitching coach (1982-84) and selected in 1985 for his 21-year major league pitching career. Barry Larkin played in two games for Nashville in 1989 on an injury rehabilitation assignment. The Reds shortstop was enshrined in 2012.

*Skeeter Barnes (1979, 88-90) and Don Mattingly (1981) are the only Sounds players to have their jersey numbers retired. Barnes wore No. 00 while Mattingly donned No. 18.

*There are 1,231 players listed on the Nashville Sounds all-time roster.

*On November 8, 2013, Nashville mayor Karl Dean announced that agreements had been reached with the State of Tennessee, the Nashville Sounds, and a leading multi-family developer for a significant public/private partnership that will allow Metro to build a new minor league ballpark near the old Sulphur Dell site in the Jefferson Street/Germantown area.

*A ceremonial groundbreaking for the new ballpark was held on the construction site on January 27, 2014.

*On April 22, 2014 the Nashville Sounds announced that First Tennessee Bank purchased the naming rights to the new ballpark. First Tennessee Park is scheduled to open in April 2015.

*On June 20, 2014 the Nashville Sounds announced that a new high definition version of its famous guitar-shaped scoreboard would be one of the signature pieces for First Tennessee Park. The scoreboard will feature an HD, LED screen that will measure 4,200 square feet making it one of the largest in minor league baseball.

*Sounds Pitcher Jimmy Nelson was selected as the PCL's Pitcher-of-the-Year for 2014. Nelson went 10-2 in 17 outings with a 1.46 ERA while striking out 114 batters in his 111 innings of work. Nelson was called up to Milwaukee on July 11.

*The Sounds hosted their final game at Greer Stadium on August 27, 2014 with an 8-5 loss to Sacramento. The sellout crowd of 11,067 witnessed Sounds reliever Rob Wooten taking the loss. Dustin Molleken worked the final one and two-thirds scoreless innings to be the last Sounds pitcher to record a pitch at Greer. Outfielder Jeremy Hermida hit the final Sounds home run and catcher Lucas May was Nashville's final batter striking out in

The "Sound Waves," the first-ever Nashville Sounds dance team, debuted in the 2016 home opener. Front row (left to right): Karli Whitson, Kayla Carolus, Amy Royer, Mackenzie Weber, Courtni Poe. Back row (left to right): Cayla Owen, Katie Crockett, Andrea Howard, Abrielle Spohr, Molli Benson. *Courtesy of the Nashville Sounds.*

the ninth inning with the bases loaded. The Oak Ridge Boys sang the final National Anthem at Greer Stadium.

*On September 18, 2014 the Sounds announced that the ball club was changing its major league affiliate from Milwaukee to Oakland, remaining in the PCL. The new Player Development Contract will run through 2018.

*The Sounds unveiled on October 9, 2014 their new logo and announced new uniforms for the 2015 season. On January 21, 2015 the Sounds revised their new logo that reverted to the classic red and black color scheme popular with Nashville Sounds fans.

*First Tennessee Park opened on April 17, 2015 with a 3-2 victory over Colorado Springs in 10 innings.

*Nashville manager Steve Scarsone is named the PCL's Manager-of-the-Year for 2016 after leading the Sounds to an American Southern Division championship and best league record (83-59).

*The Sounds, in their home opener in 2016, revealed their first-ever dance team. The "Sound Waves" performed dances between certain innings and helped with on-the-field activities with the fans.

* The Sounds announced on November 15, 1916 that Ryan Christenson would become the new Nashville manager for 2017. Rick Rodriguez will be retained as the pitching coach while Eric Martins will return as the batting coach.

Nashville Vols' Year-by-Year Results

Year	Record	Finish	Manager
1901*	78-45	1st	Newt Fisher
1902*	82-42	1st	Newt Fisher
1903	60-62	5th	Newt Fisher
1904	72-67	5th	Newt Fisher
1905	47-88	7th	Newt Fisher/Mike Finn
1906	45-92	7th	Mike Finn
1907	59-78	8th	Johnny Dobbs
1908*	75-56	1st	Bill Bernhard
1909	82-55	2nd	Bill Bernhard
1910	64-76	5th	Bill Bernhard
1911	69-64	4th	Bill Schwartz
1912	67-70	4th	Bill Schwartz
1913	62-76	7th	Bill Schwartz
1914	77-72	5th	Bill Schwartz
1915	75-78	4th	Bill Schwartz
1916*	84-54	1st	Roy Ellam
1917	77-73	5th	Roy Ellam
1918	30-40	7th	Roy Ellam
1919	55-83	8th	Roy Ellam
1920	65-89	7th	Roy Ellam
1921	62-90	6th	Hub Perdue
1922	56-96	7th	Larry Doyle
1923	75-77	6th	Jimmy Hamilton
1924	78-75	4th	Jimmy Hamilton
1925	81-72	3rd	Jimmy Hamilton

1926	83-68	4th	Jimmy Hamilton
1927	84-69	4th	Jimmy Hamilton
1928#	31-42	6th	Jimmy Hamilton
	28-52	8th	
1929	90-63	2nd	Clarence Rowland
1930	66-87	7th	Clarence Rowland
1931	51-102	8th	Joe Klugman
1932	75-78	4th	Joe Klugman/Charlie Dressen
1933#	39-37	5th	Charlie Dressen
	36-32	3rd	
1934#	46-26	1st	Charlie Dressen
	41-39	4th	Charlie Dressen
1935	82-69	4th	Frank Brazill/Lance Richbourg
1936	86-65	2nd	Lance Richbourg
1937	80-73	5th	Lance Richbourg
1938	84-66	2nd	Charlie Dressen
1939	85-68	5th	Larry Gilbert
1940*	101-47	1st	Larry Gilbert
1941	83-70	2nd	Larry Gilbert
1942	85-66	2nd	Larry Gilbert
1943**	49-26	1st	Larry Gilbert
	34-29	3rd	
1944**	32-36	5th	Larry Gilbert
	47-25	1st	
1945	55-84	7th	Larry Gilbert
1946	75-78	5th	Larry Gilbert
1947	80-73	3rd	Larry Gilbert
1948*	95-58	1st	Larry Gilbert
1949*	95-57	1st	Rollie Hemsley
1950	86-64	3rd	Don Osborn
1951	78-76	5th	Don Osborn

1952	73-79	6th	Hugh Poland
1953	85-69	2nd	Hugh Poland
1954	64-90	6th	High Poland
1955	77-74	5th	Joe Schultz
1956	75-79	7th	Ernie White
1957	83-69	3rd	Dick Sisler
1958	76-78	5th	Dick Sisler
1959	84-64	3rd	Dick Sisler
1960	71-82	6th	Jim Turner
1961	69-83	6th	Spencer Robbins
1962			No Team Fielded
1963#	24-47	8th	John Fitzpatrick
	29-39	6th	
Overall Record		4,569-4,446	

*Regular Season Champion.
**Split Season Champion.
#Split Season.

197

Nashville Sounds' Year-by-Year Results

Year	Parent Club	Record	Finish**	Manager (s)
1978	Cincinnati	64-77	9th	Chuck Goggin
1979*	Cincinnati	83-61	2nd	George Scherger
1980	New York (AL)	97-46	1st	Stump Merrill
1981	New York (AL)	81-62	1st	Stump Merrill
1982*	New York (AL)	77-67	2nd	Johnny Oates
1983	New York (AL)	88-58	2nd	Doug Holmquist
1984	New York (AL)	74-73	5th	Jim Marshall
1985	Detroit	71-70	5th	Lee Walls/Leon Roberts/Gordie MacKenzie
1986	Detroit	68-74	6th	Leon Roberts
1987	Cincinnati	64-76	7th	Jack Lind
1988	Cincinnati	73-69	4th	Jack Lind/Wayne Garland/Jim Hoff/George Scherger/Frank Lucchesi
1989	Cincinnati	74-72	4th	Frank Lucchesi
1990	Cincinnati	86-61	2th	Pete Mackanin
1991	Cincinnati	65-78	6th	Pete Mackanin
1992	Cincinnati	67-77	T-6th	Pete Mackanin/Dave Miley
1993	Chicago (AL)	81-62	2nd	Rick Renick
1994	Chicago (AL)	83-61	2nd	Rick Renick
1995	Chicago (AL)	68-76	6th	Rick Renick
1996	Chicago (AL)	77-67	4th	Rick Renick

1997	Chicago (AL)	74-67	T-3rd	Tom Spencer
1998	Pittsburgh	67-76	12th	Trent Jewett
1999	Pittsburgh	80-60	4th	Trent Jewett
2000	Pittsburgh	63-79	T-12th	Trent Jewett/ Richie Hebner
2001	Pittsburgh	64-77	13th	Marty Brown
2002	Pittsburgh	72-71	T-8th	Marty Brown
2003	Pittsburgh	81-62	2nd	Trent Jewett
2004	Pittsburgh	63-79	14th	Trent Jewett
2005*	Milwaukee	75-69	6th	Frank Kremblas
2006	Milwaukee	76-68	T-5th	Frank Kremblas
2007	Milwaukee	89-55	1st	Frank Kremblas
2008	Milwaukee	59-81	16th	Frank Kremblas
2009	Milwaukee	75-69	5th	Don Money
2010	Milwaukee	77-67	5th	Don Money
2011	Milwaukee	71-73	T-6th	Don Money
2012	Milwaukee	67-77	12th	Mike Guerrero
2013	Milwaukee	57-87	16th	Mike Guerrero/ Charlie Greene
2014	Milwaukee	77-67	6th	Rick Sweet
2015	Oakland	66-78	12th	Steve Scarsone
2016	Oakland	83-59	1st	Steve Scarsone
Overall Record		2,877-2,710		

*Denotes League Champions.
**Finish represents composite league standing.

About the Author

Bill Traughber is a researcher and writer of Nashville sports history. He is a graduate of Brentwood Academy and Aquinas Junior College (Nashville). The Nashville-born writer's work has appeared in *Athlon's Baseball Annual (1995), Nashville Sports Weekly, Titans Exclusive, Big Orange Illustrated, The City Paper, Tennessee Titans Season Review 2001-02, New York Daily News, Sports Nashville, Tennessee Sports Magazine, Williamson Herald and the National Pastime (SABR).*

His first book, *Nashville Sports History: Stories From the Stands* was published by the History Press in March 2010 and his second book, *Brentwood Academy Football, From a Cow Pasture to a Tradition, 1970-2009* was published in September 2010 by McQuiddy Classic Printing in Nashville, Tennessee. The *History Press* released a third book, *Vanderbilt Football: Tales of Commodore Gridiron History* in September 2011. A fourth *History Press* book was released in October 2012 *Vanderbilt Basketball, Tales of Commodore Hardwood History.*

Traughber's stories have also appeared in these additional publications: Nashville Sounds 2004-2014 programs; Nashville Sounds 2007-14 Media Guides; Brentwood Academy 2004-10 football programs; Vanderbilt University 2004-16 football game programs and Vanderbilt 2008-10 Baseball Media Guide. His work has appeared on several websites including nashvillesounds.com, vucommodores.com and sportsnashville.net.

Bill has been recognized as a two-time recipient of the Writer-of-the-Year award and six-time winner as Best Feature Writer as a member of the Tennessee Sports Writers Association. Traughber has won several other writing awards from that organization and has written over 200 feature stories about Nashville baseball. His passion for baseball has given him the opportunity to interview these former Nashville Vols:

Bob Lennon, Buster Boguskie, Johnny Sain, Jim O'Toole, Tommy "Buckshot" Brown, Larry Taylor, Buddy Gilbert, Bobby Durnbaugh, Jim Maloney, John Edwards, Marv Staehle, Roy Pardue, Ben Wade, Ace Adams, Arnie Moser, Jim Kirby, Tom Satriano and Ray Hamrick. Included are these former Nashville Sounds: George Weicker, Chuck Goggin, Farrell Owens (GM), Don Money, Charlie Mitchell, Rich Gale (coach), Brian Dayett, Stump Merrill, Rick Duncan, Tom Bolton, Buck Showalter, Skeeter Barnes, Gene Menees, Scotti Madison, Larry Schmittou (President) and Chuck Morgan (First PA announcer).

Bill Traughber as a Little League baseball player. *Courtesy of the author.*

And interviews with additional players with major league experience include: Enos Slaughter, Wayne Garland, Sam Ewing, George Altman, Fred Valentine, Jim Cosman, Mickey Kreitner, Jerry Bell, Chuck Meriweather (umpire), Michael Coleman, Mike Willis, David Price, Pedro Alvarez, Jeremy Sowers, Ryan Flaherty, Tony Kemp and Corban Joseph. Other baseball interviews by Traughber include Tim Corbin, Warner Jones, Elliott Jones, Roy Mewbourne, Hunter Bledsoe, Lillian Jackson (AAGBL), Butch McCord and Ken Dugan.

Traughber's memberships include the Tennessee Sports Writers Association (TSWA), Nashville Sports Council, Society of American Baseball Researchers (SABR), Football Writers Association of America (FWAA) and the Intercollegiate Football Researchers Association (IFRA).

His stories have taken him to Cooperstown, NY, Anchorage, Alaska and the White House in Washington, D.C. Traughber resides in Brentwood, Tennessee.

CPSIA information can be obtained
at www.ICGtesting.com
Printed in the USA
LVHW021416180521
687767LV00002B/252